INTIMATE LANDSCAPES

PAUL RILEY

INTIMATE LANDSCAPES

How to paint close-up views in watercolours

BROADCAST BOOKS

British Library Cataloguing in Publication Data
Riley, Paul
  Intimate landscapes: how to paint close-up views in watercolour.
  1. Watercolour paintings. Techniques
  I. Title
  751.422436

ISBN 1-85404-005-7

Published by Broadcast Books
The Old School House
The Courtyard
Bell Street
Shaftesbury
Dorset SP7 8BP

First impression 1991
Copyright © 1991 Paul Riley

Typeset by Editorial Enterprises, Torquay
Printed in Hong Kong

This book is dedicated to Milo *In Pace*

CONTENTS

INTRODUCTION

We all have a sense of place. When we emerge from our homes we are immediately confronted with the familiar. This, in fact, is our landscape. The way in which Nature and even man have contrived to unite the sky with the land below has been a source of endless fascination for painters. When I was very young I lived in a large town where my boundaries were entirely manmade. Nature could only proliferate in gardens. But fairly close to us there existed a large park where the landscape could tangle unchecked, and the changing seasons painted the land different colours. I can remember noticing with a child's eyes the small, intimate spaces in this landscape world. From such a perspective these special places provided a great deal of comfort. As an adult I have lost none of these sensations and continue to look for these quiet corners. In this book I will take you on a journey to find them; we will set up our easels and discover the joy in painting these sites.

I will be asking you to look in a special way, to look in depth and to look with a sense of adventure. The paintings will vary according to your mood, the type of weather and the seasons. Some of the information may seem quite scientific but do not let this daunt you. Painters need to analyse what they see in front of them in much the same way as the scientists. We share a fascination for what we see about us.

Painting outside can seem a daunting experience at first. You are subject to other people's curiosity, vagaries of the weather and your own sense of inadequacy. However, once Nature starts to reveal all her hidden secrets, you will find yourself in another world — a world full of surprises!

In the following pages I will introduce you to painters who felt a special affinity with the landscape. They have prepared the groundwork for us. Looking at colour, for example, would not be possible without Van Gogh and Monet; composition without Claude; or sheer courage from Turner.

Landscape painting is part concentrated mental effort and part showmanship. You have to be able to parry the inquisitive, sometimes downright aggressive spectator, but the rewards always outweigh the disadvantages. When you get home and look at your work, you realise that although it may not have captured exactly what you were after, it is so much more expressive of the moment than any snapshot. Why? Because you were there, and because you looked much harder than anyone else before you.

CHAPTER 1

PAST PRINCIPALS

I am constantly amazed at the variety of painting that has been done over the centuries. Without this heritage we would have no framework on which to hang our own ideas. One of my favourite occupations is to look at the work of different peoples from all over the world, and to read them like a book.

These paintings offer endless clues and information that inspire me and cause me to explore fresh avenues in my work. You should take this opportunity to examine just a few of these attempts at unravelling the landscape around us.

Each of these past Masters has something special to offer. They have all suffered as we have, only more so, and over a huge period of time. Their lessons are incalculable. Nature will forever teach us, but it is our past that has managed to unravel some of her secrets.

Early painters

Amber Palace, Jaipur
The painting was done on the spot in India under quite trying circumstances. Whilst trying to paint I was surrounded by a multitude of onlookers. I have attempted to put down patches of colour in the same jewel-like way that the Indians use. The painting is on handmade paper produced nearby, and made from rags gathered by the local rag pickers. There are many fine pieces of silk and detritus embedded in the paper itself. It is extremely absorbent and I had to use very fine, quick strokes.

Landscape painting is a relatively recent innovation. The earliest painters had a function to depict the activity of their elders and betters in a society of hunter-gatherers. Much of human life was shown, with the landscape as purely an adjunct to the main activity; it was there simply to indicate location. Painters from certain countries also depicted emperors, queens, and courtiers dallying in their palaces. Here the landscape served to add a decorative background to their frivolity.

The Chinese painters were among the first to use the landscape as an end in itself, to relay feelings of tranquillity and calmness. Water

played a significant role. In fact the Chinese were the first exponents of the use of watercolour as we know it today. However, many of their techniques and methods of handling the subject matter were quite different from what we in the Western world know as landscape painting. For example, the paper they used was highly absorbent and required extremely rapid handling. Every touch had to work. It meant therefore that the painter had to be highly skilled before committing himself to a large work. The format was usually upright, and the painting executed on a roll of paper. This suited their particular landscape

Squirrels on a Plane Tree
Mogul c1615
A considerable amount of fine detail is incorporated in this painting. The method of applying the paint is by way of fine marmot or squirrel-hair brushes using an almost gouache kind of watercolour pigment.

The design of the painting is very much in pattern form, with the tree introduced as a silhouette against a gold sky. Although the painting is about an incident — a hunt — the landscape plays a considerable part.

interest — often mountain scenery — and also enabled them to incorporate poems alongside the picture using their vertical script.

Indian painters worked in a very different manner. I have watched painters at work in Jaipur using the same methods as their Mogul ancestors centuries before. They adopt an opaque method of watercolour painting. I have seen them crushing semi-precious stones — lapis lazuli for blue, and moonstone for white — into a fine powder, then mixing this with gum arabic to form a very fine paste rather like a gouache mixture. This was applied to a smooth paper — often vellum taken from old books — using extremely fine brushes. The paper had been given a preparatory white ground for working on. The result was a jewel-like painting with intricate detail and brilliant colouring. Quite often gold was applied to enhance this effect.

The difference between the two techniques — Chinese and Indian — is that the Chinese employ a transparent use of watercolour, whereas in Indian painting it is more opaque. In this book you will see that both of these techniques have been used.

Watercolour painting in the West only really developed in the eighteenth and nineteenth centuries. Prior to this the medium was only used either for illustration or as a preparation for works in other media, such as oil or tempera. Monks used a gouache type of watercolour in their illuminated manuscripts, similar to the Mogul painters. They included marvellous examples of landscape in their scriptures.

The early Renaissance painters occasionally used monochrome watercolour, generally bistre, for cartoons. Their breadth of handling was fresh and quite up-to-date.

Dürer was perhaps the first Western painter who was able to exploit the medium as an end in itself. He produced landscapes in watercolour that successfully portrayed all the nuances of atmosphere.

Claude Lorraine

The importance of Claude Lorraine (1600–82) is relative to his sense of composition. He was a romantic painter and much of his subject matter centred around classical mythology. Although he was primarily an oil painter, his technique and handling of colour are very relevant to watercolourists.

Most of his paintings portrayed a subject or story to which the landscape — frequently imaginary — was merely a setting. He would take sketches from real locations and then compose these, using a structural device of his own making to produce allegorical paintings. The structure consisted of using an approximate one-third/two-thirds system. This meant dividing the picture plane in such a way as to produce such proportions, commonly referred to as a 'golden section device'.

In Claude's paintings you will see that he has incorporated a large mass of either trees, rocks or buildings to one side, with a fairly low horizon line. Then to counterbalance on the other side he painted trees or groups of trees, or buildings, silhouetted against the sky. He used subtly balanced tonal gradations executed in a very delicate way.

He was noted for creating strong atmosphere in his paintings, and over the years this has been the source of much frustration among artists who have attempted similar techniques. His compositional devices are still used today by many

David at the Cave of Abdullam
Claude Lorraine 1600–82
Using the sketch opposite one can see how this painting was composed. The story has been incorporated in the work, but the main emphasis is on the landscape which would have been fictional. Note the subtle gradations of cool colours in the distance moving towards warmth in the foreground, thereby creating a wonderful depth to the painting.

In this sketch I have shown how the painting has been subdivided in terms of the golden section. You will note from the brackets that the small part of the picture as it intersects the side is in proportion to the large — as the large section is in direct ratio to the whole side. Arriving at this proportion should be a matter of instinct rather than calculation and many landscape painters use this method.

landscape painters, because his paintings strike a harmonious balance with the various elements within the landscape. If his techniques are followed too slavishly a painting can appear a little obvious. However, as in all things, when true harmony is achieved the painting will work.

Claude did not paint watercolours in polychrome but produced many that are referred to as watercolour drawings. These were invariably preparations for his oil paintings. His method of handling the watercolour was fascinating because of the way in which he was able to render trees and the light reflected from them.

Usually his technique involved the use of pen and brown ink, with tints of watercolour in grey or brown

applied with a brush. Some of the darkest tones would be applied by the use of black chalk, with highlights added in white chalk. This technique was used by many earlier painters, notably Leonardo da Vinci who handled this most complex of media in a magical way.

You will find that combining other media to reinforce your watercolours will add a new dimension to your work. Incorporating pen work, for example, particularly if using watercolour instead of ink, will add to the detailed structure in a painting. Chalk or pastels will create subtle highlights which can be blended much in the same way as the watercolour. Adding pastel can give body to your painting.

Joseph Mallord William Turner

Turner (1775–1851) was a great fan of Claude Lorraine, and quite often attempted compositions closely akin to his. At the beginning Turner followed Claude's mode of story-telling, but this soon changed and he painted landscapes in their own right.

His stature as a watercolourist in England was immense. He introduced many innovative ideas in both handling and subject matter. For example, one of his methods of capturing light and atmosphere was to produce what he called 'colour beginnings'. These were almost abstract conglomerations of colour, done on the spot in often quite difficult circumstances. Contained in small sketch-books, these give the watercolourist a fascinating insight into Turner's methods of working.

He would sometimes use additives in his colours in order to produce specific textures — soap and flour paste, for example. He would attack the surface with all manner of instruments to create textural variations, and he even grew his thumb-nail long for this purpose.

Turner also employed innovative methods for producing light in his paintings. He would use a pen with water in it to work over light areas, or areas to be lightened, and then raise the colour thus dampened with blotting paper. Breadcrumbs were also used to absorb patches of pigment from the surface of the paper — again to produce light.

Lake Nemi
J.M.W. Turner 1775–1851
This is a classic example of a watercolour work by Turner. It shows his breadth of handling. Notice that stippling has been used to create details. Scratching out and absorbing colour have been used to produce highlights.

His device for creating depth is similar to Claude's, with the use of blue in the distance and warm browns in the foreground. To create the silhouette of the trees, light against the background, he would have employed what I call negative painting, which is leaving the white of the paper behind in order to create the tree form. Some of this negative work would been done by erasing the paint from the surface as described in the text.

Dittisham Mill creek

A view of this nature offers the painter the opportunity to explore the subtle nuances of tone. This is particularly appropriate to watercolours and Turner was its best exponent. In order to paint this scene I had to examine the delicate shades of reflected light that came from both sky and trees. The mud of the river bed was a series of pale pinks which had to describe not only the form of the banks but also their texture. In controlling these subtle tints I examined how Turner would have handled them. The general idea behind the painting, that of creating a romantic mood, also owes much to Turner's way of seeing his landscapes.

This method of painting, which extends the simple use of the brush, lends a particularly dynamic force to his work. The lessons for the watercolourist are great as they extend our repertoire considerably. Inventiveness of this nature is essential to give our work greater force and mystery. In looking at Turner's paintings one is often dumbfounded as to how some of the marks have been achieved.

Turner was a great advocate of the *plein air* form of painting, which meant going out into the landscape and recording that which Nature provides. He would go to any lengths to capture a nuance of light or atmosphere. You will find that if you follow his example no matter how insignificant your marks may be they will give strength to your work. These notes can always be added to a picture in the studio.

Turner was working during a period of great scientific and industrial development, and became greatly imbued with the zeal for experiment that attracted his generation. One of his preoccupations was examining colour, and he was influenced by Goethe's treatise on colour theory. His experiments preceded those of the Impressionists who also looked at the scientific analysis of colour. Even today our knowledge of how the eye perceives colour and its interpretation by the brain is being researched.

One particular way of seeing colour differently is to see the landscape in a 'foreign' light. When Turner travelled south to Italy he noticed the relative clarity of the colours compared to England. This experience refreshed his palette and enabled him to see his home landscape with renewed eyes.

Vincent Van Gogh

Van Gogh (1853–90) was a very passionate painter in oils. His relevance to watercolourists may seem a little unclear, but he offers us the opportunity for extending our watercolour technique.

Van Gogh developed his skill through his close contact with the Impressionists. The colour used by Monet and Gauguin enriched his palette. The techniques and theories of the Pointillist Seurat altered his brushwork. His work culminated in a powerful textural quality where the colour intertwined all the elements of a landscape — the sky and the land.

The Pointillist technique was developed as a way of introducing patches of colour that when viewed from a distance would merge and form a secondary colour, for example small particles of yellow intermixed with small dots of blue would blend and form a green.

Van Gogh extended this further by using striations of paint that

Meadow with butterflies
Vincent Van Gogh 1853–90
Although this is an oil painting, it offers many suggestions to the watercolourist. The very simple subject — a small patch of ground — is seen in a very intimate way. It is in fact an excuse for a variety of brush strokes, some very short, some long, which weave a pattern of texture over the entire canvas.

The watercolourist can employ the same technique using brushes of differing widths.

Sunflowers in the Gironde

The method of handling the paint in this picture is very akin to Van Gogh's oil-painting techniques. A lot of white paper is allowed to shine through, surrounding each brush stroke with white light. Although certain wash areas are evident, these are counterbalanced by stripes of colour which add variety to otherwise flat areas.

I have allowed the sky to weave in with the landscape, very much in the way that Van Gogh would have done.

wove through the canvas, creating other harmonies. Up until the Impressionists the watercolourist's palette had been restricted to blues and earth colours. To some degree Turner had extended this, and many consider him to be the father of the Impressionists. Van Gogh, however, produced colour in an unlimited and impassioned style, which serves to enrich the watercolourist's way of looking at the landscape. I sometimes use Van Gogh's method to

give excitement and movement to areas in my landscape painting.

This technique is very useful when working on site in wet weather, as waiting for paint to dry can take some time. Placing colour in stripes, with small sections of white paper surrounding them, enables you to cover the surface area rapidly. I generally use an absorbent paper which takes the colour more rapidly. Try this technique for yourself, using colour in an uninhibited manner.

Paul Cézanne

The Winding Road
Paul Cézanne 1839–1906
In this painting nothing is 'literally' painted ie the grass and the leaves do not look like grass and leaves! Patches of colour have been laid to produce the forms as they interlock with each other.

It is interesting to note that Cézanne (1839–1906) produced the greatest number of watercolours among the Impressionists. Many of these were preparations for his oil paintings. However, lots of them were done out of sheer pleasure. He would produce these *en plein air* on the site, and they were generally exhaustive studies of a particular corner of a landscape.

One of Cézanne's favourite themes was Mont St Victoire near Aix-en-Provence. This mountain allowed him to explore one of his more perplexing problems — his expression of outline. He felt that to state the outline of an object was to fix it too solidly in the mind's eye. Instead, he preferred to infer it by a

multiplicity of strokes, thereby weaving it into the background. This gave his work a shimmering quality. He also investigated the shapes of the spaces left behind by objects. These areas appeared to him to have a form as significant and solid as the objects they revealed.

Cézanne was mostly concerned with the investigation of such phenomena, rather than trying to paint a picture in its own right. His technique required the use of a rather limited palette of colours. These were usually laid in a thin, transparent manner, using quite a broad brush. Outlines were broken so that the colour veils could intersect from background to object, thereby harmonising the whole.

Another aspect of Cézanne's work involved the exploration of rhythms in the landscape. These rhythms, as in music, involved the use of line curves which echoed and re-echoed throughout the painting. When noting a particular slant of a tree trunk, for example, he would find a similar angle in another aspect of the picture. These rhythms were also included in his use of colour, and he permeated the picture plane with patches of the same colour tc draw the painting together and make it whole.

Most of Cézanne's painting was dominated by his concern with form. The exploration of form overrode his interest in colour. The fascinating thing is that when he saw a

mass of foliage, his thought was not for the individual leaves, but for the overall shape or form in relation to the tree trunks or sky.

This structured approach to landscape painting enables you to become less inhibited about the detail. You need to look for the underlying form to understand how the landscape fits together, rather like a jigsaw puzzle. This is useful when analysing how sections of the painting interlock with each other; for example, the shape of the sky around the mountain's profile, and the forms within the mountain broken up by rock structures. These in turn would interlock with the profile of trees, and so on. Looking at your landscape as a jigsaw pattern helps to break down the seemingly complex issue into much more simple forms.

Mont Ventou
The lessons of Cézanne are evident in this painting, in which I have tried to give form to these mountains. The difficulty lies firstly in creating depth, and secondly in analysing the way the mountain would integrate with both the foreground and the sky. Edges have become lost to allow the merging to take place. Like Cézanne I have allowed patches of colour to merge around the painting to give it unity, using warm blues and violets.

Sketches, Mont St Victoire
Here are two sketches, taken from the same view, of the mountain that was of such interest to Cézanne. On this particular day I wanted to explore the form in the way he did, and note how this could change according to one's point of view.

The simple patches of colours attempt to reduce an otherwise complex scene to a straightforward series of colour areas.

Nature of influence

We are fortunate in having such a varied past to draw from. The number of painters with varying techniques has provided us with a rich source of inspiration.

To a large extent all painting is a synthesis of the past. By this I mean it would be impossible for us to paint without some knowledge of what has been done before. In many respects painting is like a series of building blocks, comprising different methods of approach, different subject matter and different techniques, with which we can develop our own way of interpreting what we see.

All painters in their formative development seek information from artists they admire and with whose techniques they are in sympathy. It is always a good form of training for the hand and the eye to copy some of these past Masters.

I have visited several of the places that the famous names have worked in. I was able to absorb the atmosphere and feel the inspiration that stimulated the painter at that time. These exercises enable you to look with new eyes at your own surroundings, which will give a fresh stimulation to your work.

It may surprise you that I have suggested looking at other mediums for developing your watercolours, but this is something I have done many times when trying to advance my way of seeing. With its density of colour, oil painting in particular serves to enrich the power of watercolours. The differences in mediums and in the ways of thinking between, say, the West and the Orient, also serve to change and develop your views.

Students often complain that when painting a landscape they are confronted with so much green that they do not know how to separate it all. In looking at the way in which other painters handle this seeming mass of unchecked colour, you will discover that they have developed devices for overcoming the problem. For example, in a Constable painting you will note that very little green has been used when portraying a large area of trees. Browns, golds and even reds appear among the green to relieve the picture of any sense of tedium. Bonnard, who enjoyed painting aspects of his garden, used colour in a particularly expressive way,

employing practically every other hue but green. Broken colour in the Impressionists' style has been particularly useful to the watercolourist in helping to relieve the boredom of flat areas of wash.

Wherever you can, try to see your favourite painter's work.

These pictures will have a specific quality related to the actual material upon which they are painted. You will be able to see the way in which the surface has been treated. Also note the density of colour, how much or how little has been applied, and the way in which the

painting has been constructed.

The three most important things to look for when analysing the work of another painter are composition, colour and subject matter. Composition is the way the picture has been arranged, and past Masters have used many devices in their exploration of assembling the component parts. Some of these techniques will help to trigger your responses. Look at Indian paintings for pattern harmonies, and Turner for abstraction. You will discover colour in all its variety by looking at Bonnard, Vuillard and Monet. The subject matter need not be obvious. I have seen beautifully simple watercolours by Sargent of fruit on a tree, which demonstrates that subject matter is all around us.

Drawing on sources from the past helps us to appreciate the vast range of ideas that permeated art history; ideas about the ways in which we see. Perspective, for example, was different in other parts of the world and has been viewed in various ways throughout history. What may seem obvious to us now was not always so. We still have the opportunity to open the eyes of others to the world around us.

Lily pond with willow
One of my favourite painters is Claude Monet, who did for colour what the wheel did for transport. He was able to break down a simple green and demonstrate the myriad colours within it. This gave his work an illusive, shimmering quality. In my painting I have sought to emulate this breakdown process. I often refer to my subject matter as an excuse for colour. This means that the willow is really only painted in order to explore reds, oranges and yellows — the water and lilies serve to examine blues, greens and violets. I then try to seek out the relationship between the two ranges of colours.

CHAPTER 2

SKETCHING FROM NATURE

At one time I worked in an office and used to dream of finding myself buried in the landscape simply painting. The joy of being in a tranquil environment, with only my thoughts, is something very hard to communicate.

Most novice landscape painters have a fear of actually starting, but there are a few devices on hand to help overcome this problem.

Some form of planning is required to get you going. This does not need to be laboured, but it can be fun. Sketching from nature is the best way of breaking down the barrier between the hand and the eye.

In some parts of the world, notably the Orient, people are more contemplative of nature. Although our first thoughts may be our best, they must be allowed to consolidate.

The window

Imagine you are in a field surrounded by a subject you wish to explore. It looks perfect. But is it? A normal reaction is simply to set up your easel, and start straightaway. The drawback with this is that you may build in mistakes which will be hard to rectify at a later stage in your painting. There may be elements within the landscape that do not necessarily accord with your ideal.

The first requirement is to make some decisions. What format are you going to adopt — vertical or horizontal? Make a 'window' by cutting out a rectangular shape in a piece of paper or card that corresponds in proportion to your final painting. The overall size of this window need be no more than 8in (200mm) by 6in (150mm). Decide on your subject matter, then look through the window at eye-level. Extend your arm, and you will note that the further away the window is from your eye the smaller the scene appears, and the nearer to your eye, the larger the scene. The frame of the window cancels out that area of the landscape that is superfluous.

You can determine whether the composition would work best vertically or horizontally. It is a wise precaution to mark the edges of your window at the half-way points and quarter points to help transfer the design to your painting. When looking through the window you can see where the main intersections of

your composition lie. The horizon line, for example, will relate to these indicator marks on your window. All that is required to transfer the design is a few light dots in very pale watercolour on your painting, to indicate where these main intersection points occur. If you make a mistake it is easy to erase the dots with a little water. In fact, many of these marks can simply be painted over in a stronger tone as your composition develops.

As you become practised with this method other techniques can be used: simply masking with the hands will give enough indication as to what viewpoint you want to

adopt. A further sophistication could be to use your camera's viewfinder to achieve a similar effect; and if you have a polaroid camera, a quick snap of the view will help in deciding whether or not you have arrived at a satisfactory composition.

It is often a good idea to do what I call a small 'thumbnail' sketch of the view seen through the window, preparatory to committing yourself to the painting. This sketch will solidify your ideas and iron out any of the complications that are likely to exist in the scene before you. Keeping the sketch small does away with the tendency to become over-detailed at too early a stage.

This photograph shows the full extent of the landscape under consideration. I have superimposed a window to give an indication of the zone I wish to paint. It is possible that another artist would have chosen a different view. This is very much a question of personal choice.

The window is marked to indicate centre points.

Here I have noted the main intersection points: horizontally, the junction of the water to the land, and the hills to the sky; vertically, the positioning of the boats and the cottage. This sketch of necessity is very simple and is intended only for layout purposes.

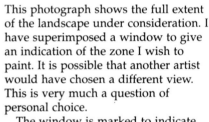

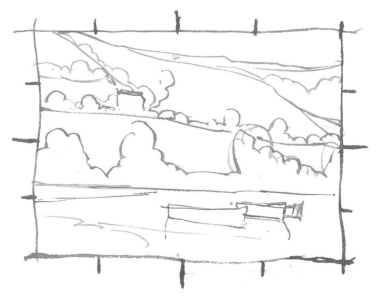

1 After a preliminary drawing-in, the main washes are laid to provide mood. I am using a large sable brush for this purpose and flood much of the colour, allowing one to merge into the other. Drawing is done very lightly in a pale blue colour.

2 The main focus in this painting is the group of boats in the foreground. I have taken a very condensed view and used reflections to provide specific interest. A second relay of washes is now superimposed on the first to give added depth but without tightening up too much and losing the atmosphere.

3 There comes a stage in a painting where a certain amount of detail has to be established in order for the picture to have interest. Here I am using a flat brush to indicate the trees on the far bank. I am constantly attracted to fleeting reflections of light, such as the shadows cast by the trees on the horizon, and record these as they occur.

The time factor

You have sat down and produced some sketches. A few colour notes later, you prepare your palette before settling on the final painting. You look up, and what has happened? The scene has shifted, the light has changed, clouds have moved. What can you do to control this? Monet, the Impressionist painter, was acutely aware of the time factor and produced a series of paintings which attempted to pin this problem down. He noted that as the sun went round, certain reflective elements in the landscape would change colour considerably. This factor affects landscape painting when done in the field.

There are two ways to overcome this problem. The first, like Monet, is to paint a series of pictures over several days, at specific points during the day. This works well if you have plenty of time at your disposal.

The second system necessitates freezing time. What factors are likely to be affected by time? If you are doing a waterscape which is subject to tides you may find that your water has disappeared entirely! The sun moves round throwing up different shadow patterns. The sky also is affected radically in that clouds are never stationary. These three factors can have a very dramatic effect during the time it takes to produce a painting. So how do we hold time? The important thing is to produce a preliminary sketch that will decide, for example, how the cloud forms are going to relate best to the painting you have designed.

Noting where the sun is in relation to your view and indicating this at the initial stage of your painting will help keep the shadows constant. In the case of water, it is extremely important to establish where the tideline is. Water

In the final painting, which was interrupted by rain, I have drawn all the details together. As can be seen by the two photographs taken at the commencement and completion of the painting, a considerable amount of memory had to be exercised. The sky is different, the tide has receded and the boats are in a different position. It meant planning the picture with the water and the boats first. The completion of the picture therefore centred on areas which were

itself may change in that it may be still and tranquil at one time and then become ruffled and agitated by the wind whilst you are painting. This will greatly affect the character of your painting. Notes on your preferred outlook are essential.

One of the most awkward things is where you have a detail, or even a focal point, which simply sails away, thereby robbing your picture of the whole reason for its existence! An early detail sketch would solve this problem. This sketch must also include colour notes to establish those elements that may escape your memory when coming to complete the picture.

Time has yet another trick in store. You may be working in a sunny situation whilst storm clouds are creeping up behind you and, needless to say, a sudden downpour wrecks any attempt at watercolour painting. In this instance, provided you have enough preliminary information, you can simply pack up and finish the painting in the studio.

The obvious *aide-mémoire* to freezing time is the camera. A slight drawback is that you have to wait for the film to be developed — another trick of time. A polaroid is useful. I tend to mistrust photographs because they do not capture some of the more delicate effects of time that you can incorporate in your picture without making it look frozen. For example, the sudden extraordinary effects of light which are only momentary can be caught in your painting as you choose. However, a photograph is useful for detail information. The fact that time can alter the scene before you so rapidly is useful in that it offers endless opportunities for exploring the same subject.

not likely to move or be radically affected by the light, for example, the form of the trees and buildings on the hillside. During the painting, certain changes of light occurred which were pinned down as the work progressed — such as the light through the trees and the reflections on the water.

Controlling time in this way can be a source of intellectual pleasure, but should not be attempted by the faint-hearted.

Composition

Having selected your view there comes a stage in your planning when composition must be considered. I have prepared a series of diagrams which reveal some 'tricks of the trade', and which will help you to achieve pleasing arrangements.

The word 'composition' fundamentally means organising your space. The purpose of this is to achieve balance. It is evident that if a portion of the painting attracts the eye to the detriment of the rest then balance has not been achieved. It is better to distribute the areas of interest around the picture, culminating in the focal point.

Primitive painters tended to divide their pictures in half, thereby creating very symmetrical designs. The difficulty with this is that the eye is not certain where to rest. Small points, such as the establishment of the horizon, are crucial in achieving the correct sense of balance. Ultimately the aim of this balancing act is to create variety for the eye to explore. Any needless repetition in the size or colour of objects

Above I have shown two discs: one black, one white. They are both the same size and it is evident that the eye is more attracted to the dark disc which is to the left of the piece of paper. This results in an imbalance.

Centre The dark disc has been reduced in size and the white enlarged in order to redress the balance.

Below We have simple discs of black and white of various sizes and number and have allowed some of them to intersect the edge of the paper, and in this way we have attempted to achieve a portion of balance. This is similar to how we see the distribution of details and tonal contrasts in a painting, and the method by which calm and active areas can be controlled.

or even marks will tend to bore the viewer's eye.

Another important aspect of composition is the point at which the major lines intersect the edge of your picture. The way in which these are angled helps draw the eye in towards your focal point, which is most significant. The focal point should not necessarily be in the centre of the picture, although it can be. The eye needs to be gently engineered to this point rather than taken directly, for fear of making the picture be too obvious. In some cases the picture can in fact have a secondary or supportive focal point. This will allow the eye to drift backwards and forwards and pick up other aspects of the picture.

Composing also centres on which areas of the painting need to be calm and which areas active. Calm areas are where the paint is free of any sudden tonal changes or incidents, active areas are where there is a great deal of tonal contrast and variety in the placing of marks. If the whole painting is active then the viewer can feel agitated to the point of not really enjoying what he is looking at. A calm area gives balance and somewhere for the eye to rest.

Composition can be likened to cooking where the balance of ingredients is extremely important. A pinch of salt may be all that is required to make your painting magical.

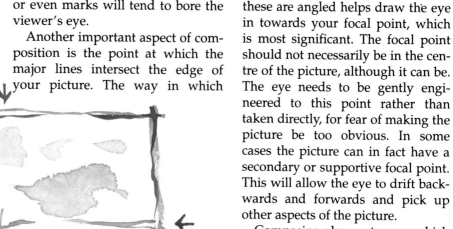

Above We see where the composition has divided the picture in half, producing a symmetry which is hard and which can appear obvious. If you have a road in your painting, leading off at the corners, the tendency is for these lines to act as an arrow, pulling you out of the picture plane.

Centre We have reduced the horizon line lower and put our centre of interest slightly to one side.

Below I have shown where principal lines have intersected the edge of the picture plane. These act as directional inferences to pull the eye towards the focal point. Note that these intersections occur at differing areas around the edges of the picture so that one is not directly opposite another.

The selection process

An extension of the composition in a painting is the selection process. This is a case of what to leave in or out. The choice is entirely up to the painter and we are fortunate in not having the limitations of the cameraman who has to wait for a specific time of day, or perhaps has to include some undesirable elements, in order to get his shot. Nobody is really going to check whether a tree is 100yd to the right or the left, or an extra few feet higher or lower, in your particular viewpoint. To some extent we call this artistic licence; it enables us to force the landscape to our will. It is at this point that the difference between what we see and what we interpret is made manifest. In painting you are expressing your own point of view, and this is what gives the picture your personal character.

The first question to ask yourself is what the painting is going to be about, and you must stick to this strongly. It could concentrate on a particular object or a certain light condition. The weather may play an important part and this must be emphasised. I exhort many of my students to highlight that which attracts them rather than attempt to record everything that exists in front of them. You may need to experiment and invent certain techniques in order to create, for example, specific textures, or a particular colour to permeate the entire picture. For this purpose I sometimes have beside me a small piece of paper so that I can play on it.

In many a landscape situation it is a case of avoiding the obvious. To do this you need to contemplate your landscape before making any form of commitment; after a while the eye will notice far more than at the initial, casual glance.

The vertical, or portrait, format has certain uses for the landscape painter.

In this instance, the layout allows the artist to explore the reflections in the water, which pick up the colouring of the foliage and the house in the background. It also enables you to highlight the powerful vertical emphasis of the mass of trees in the background.

Below is a more classic landscape format, where the flat planes of the water can be fully exploited. The viewpoint of the house in the background is, to some extent, lost amidst the foliage. For this particular landscape a horizontal format is not perhaps appropriate. Always explore both formats before any decisions are made.

House at Giverny
The house and studios at Giverny are where Monet lived and worked for the greater part of his life. It is a very beautiful place, famous for its lily-ponds, and I have visited it several times. I had wanted to do a painting which reflected the way in which Monet lived, and which at the same time conveyed his passion for water. For this reason I chose a vertical format so that both the water lilies and his home could be accommodated. I was able to investigate the reflections of the green foliage which complemented the pink hues of the house. The painting was deliberately kept very free with the exception of the house — this was handled in a different manner so that it contrasted with the foliage.

Drawing techniques

When I am 'drawing-in' I start tentatively, with a few dots determining how wide or high or long certain objects are within the composition; for example, a horizon line, where the focal point lies, and so on. This is done in a combination of ways, employing various drawing techniques. The most common is line. But line should not be seen as a piece of bent wire holding tight a particular object. It can show rhythm and movement, for example.

When watercolour painting, I generally apply line in a light colour, using a brush. The line is then invariably broken, tentatively encapsulating areas first and then working towards small detail sections where necessary. The colour can vary depending upon the subject matter; blues for trees and ground, oranges where the trees change colour, yellows where certain greens need to be

Line work serves merely to indicate the disposition of the masses in the composition. It will vary from dots to dashes to whole lines, at the same time attempting to express some kind of movement and activity rather than a static quality. Various colours have also been introduced in order to give life to the drawing.

Generally a tonal sketch of this kind would be done by way of a preliminary drawing. It is possible, however, to use these tones and place fine glazes of colour to produce a finished picture. When designing the colour these tonal contrasts should be in the back of the mind.

delineated. The tone used is always lighter than the final finished painting so that the line is ultimately masked.

Line can at times be employed in the latter stage of painting to produce definition.

Another drawing element is tone. These are the gradations of light and dark in a painting.

In Cézanne's paintings we are acutely aware of how he drew in colour. Colour is an inseparable part of drawing. In colour analysis one is not only looking for the tonal contrasts, but also for its relative intensity. When designing, this intensity generates depth in the painting.

The junction between two colours is what we might term the 'edge'. This edge is in effect a line, but it can vary from something quite crisp, with a strong tonal contrast, to extremely faint and hazy. The latter could be achieved whilst working wet-into-wet.

There will be a stage in your painting when you reach a complicated section. What is required here is a form of detail analysis. For example, there may be a boat in the foreground or a group of buildings in the middle distance. We need to know the disposition elements, such as windows, or fittings on a boat, and for this a detailed drawing may be necessary. In order not to lose affinity with watercolour I tend to do these in a fine brush. Drawing, therefore, is pulling all these elements together to provide a scheme which will enable the painting to work.

It is a pleasurable process which gives strength to the final result.

A colour sketch is not intended to be descriptive in any detailed sense. It shows the kind of colour to be used and its relative intensity. At this stage it can be decided whether the picture is going to be about greens or reds or golds. This will also attempt to establish the mood of the painting.

This shows the kind of intense study required for a complicated area. A detail analysis can be done either purely in line, in tone or in colour (if, for example, your object of interest is likely to disappear at any moment). If drawn in, line colour notes can be written in order to supplement the information.

Depth

One of the most amazing and satisfying things in all forms of painting is the way in which you can produce a hole in your paper. This is in fact an illusion. What we are doing is working on a two-dimensional surface, and attempting to create a third dimension. To achieve this effect various devices are employed to provide what we call depth. This illusion of depth is very important in landscape painting because we are dealing with a variety of subjects, occupying an area of either several square yards or several hundred square miles. Obviously the greater the distance, the greater the illusion of depth required. Even where the distance involved is only a matter of inches, the same principles apply.

There are several components to analyse, and all these relate to the way in which we handle the materials and the choice of colour. To start with it is self-evident that the fur-

ther away an object is the smaller it appears to the eye, and hence the nearer the larger. We refer to this illusion as perspective, which is analysed in more depth in Chapter 3. In a completely organic type of painting which does not contain manmade objects perspective is still evident. The picture should be divided into a series of planes which recede into the distance. These planes vary in intensity and edge. Quite often an element is introduced into a picture in order to give it a sense of scale. This may be a figure or tree, something which the observer is likely to relate to in terms of size and which will therefore give him an understanding of how far away an object or space may be. Even the sky has perspective; clouds have larger mass forms overhead and diminish in size and intensity as they reach the horizon.

The next most important element in creating depth is that of colour.

Generally speaking because the atmosphere contains water, the light waves from distant objects are split up and reduce the colour to the cooler (bluer) end of the spectrum. Colour in the foreground appears brighter and more obvious. For instance the leaves on a tree in the far distance will seem to be almost blue, whereas in the foreground they will appear much more green. The tonal contrast alters in a similar way. In the distance the tones are lighter and more closely related. As they advance towards the foreground the contrast becomes more marked, with very light tones adjacent to dark ones. Utilising this effect creates a sense of depth almost immediately.

The final most important ingredient is 'focus'. Imagine you are looking through a camera — you will tend to focus onto the object of your interest. Other parts of the picture will appear to be out of focus, and

In this sketch I have shown where the landscape can be divided into planes to create a sense of depth. These interlock and zigzag across the paper, implying the perspective necessary to make the picture work. Notice also that the sky is treated in a similar manner.

In this sketch blue has been used to indicate the far distance, with heightened colour contrast in the middle distance to create interest. The foreground has been treated very simply to attract the eye to the focal point.

the junction between two colour elements will be slightly blurred. This area is, as previously described, the edge junction. In watercolour this can be exploited to a great degree; whilst the paint is wet any colour on it will tend to bleed, and the amount of time that the paint has been allowed to dry will affect the extent of the bleeding. Therefore in the far distance colours can be placed with a considerable amount of bleed; as the subject reaches the middle distance the edges can become more distinct.

Do not allow the foreground to become too dominant with too much contrast. This may detract from your centre of interest, which usually occurs in the middle distance.

This is especially true of any vista you may attempt. When looking into intimate corners the foreground may perhaps be a mixture of leaves. This can be reduced to a pattern and used to draw attention to an object and arrest the viewer's interest.

Keep the foreground very simple, and in some instances see it merely as a form of introduction to the picture as a whole.

Aspiring to produce depth in a painting is one of the great challenges for a painter. It provides endless fascination, and it is well worth studying the methods by which

River pontoons
Cool colours dominate the distance in this painting. The tonal contrasts increase towards the foreground. The up-ended dinghies on the pontoon form the centre of interest. These have been treated very simply with strong tonal contrast. The foreground serves merely as an adjunct to this focal point; the brushwork is designed simply to draw the eye toward the pontoon.

other painters have achieved this illusion. Depth is also related to form in the sense that the landscape could be seen as a solid in the same way as a vase, and must be considered as such in order to make the picture work.

CHAPTER 3

PERSPECTIVE PRINCIPLES

Newcomers to watercolour painting may be forgiven for thinking that the subject of perspective is both complex and bewildering. It is in fact where science meets art. It is one of the techniques used to express depth in a picture, and is therefore vital in landscape painting. Basically, if we look at any scene from a particular position, subjects within the scene will reduce in size the further away they are.

Perspective can be enjoyable, and in the following pages I have described various ways of using it to enhance your work.

One-point perspective

Indian village, Rajasthan
In this picture the buildings to the right conform to the principle of one-point perspective. The painting had to be executed very rapidly, but all windows and doors, relative to the walls, converge approximately to a spot on my eye-level when extended towards the horizon.

When including buildings in your landscape, you will notice certain lines that appear to be running at awkward angles to each other. This phenomenon is what we know as 'perspective'. It was first observed and used a very long time ago, but the actual science of perspective was drawn up only relatively recently, with simple rules that could be applied in painting. These guidelines, however, must not be followed slavishly, or else your paintings may appear rather stilted. But a sense of perspective is very important.

To understand the meaning of one-point, or single-point, perspec-tive, imagine that you are standing in a completely flat landscape, on a road which disappears into the horizon. As you look at the road you will see that it is quite wide where you are, but that it becomes narrower as it recedes into the dis-tance, until finally the sides merge on the horizon as a mere dot. If you had a pencil protruding from between your eyes while looking straight down the road, this dot would be exactly on the tip of your pencil. The fact that the road appears to come from this single point is the principle of one-point perspective: all lines leading away from you, assuming a fixed eye-level, converge at a single dot.

Your physical position, and therefore your eye-level, will affect your view, and will influence the apparent angle of the sides of the road. If you were to sit down, or even lie down, these angles would appear completely different because your eye-level had lowered. The position of your head determines the exact point from which these lines emanate.

This type of perspective is quite straightforward, and is often used in paintings where the eye is lead down a street with buildings on either side. It is also employed when a building is seen straight on — a square wall, for example, with buildings coverging on either side.

To make this kind of perspective work you have to accept that your field of vision — the landscape area seen in front of you (peripheral vision) — is about 60 degrees. If you move your head from side to side over a wider angle than this, the lines would appear distorted and bent.

Single-point perspective is also used when buildings are positioned at subtle angles to one another, or if a road twists and turns. The diagram here should help to explain this. The vanishing point would move along your eye-level. Where a wall adjacent to you is disappearing towards the horizon, note that the lines of all the elements within the wall — windows, doors, sills — also converge towards the same point.

If you are trying to show a road that runs up- and downhill, this point can also move up or down vertically. This can be displayed by turning this book at right-angles, and looking at the diagram of the shifting point.

To establish the gable end on a building in perspective it is necessary to first draw two diagonals as shown on the diagram in order to find the centre line. The height of the gable is determined by eye. The same principle applies for an arch.

In order to get to grips with this form of perspective, I suggest you try a few doodles based on these diagrams, followed up by some research on site. Experiment by standing up to obtain one kind of eye-level, and then sit down and note the changes in perspective. Start simply with a road leading away from you.

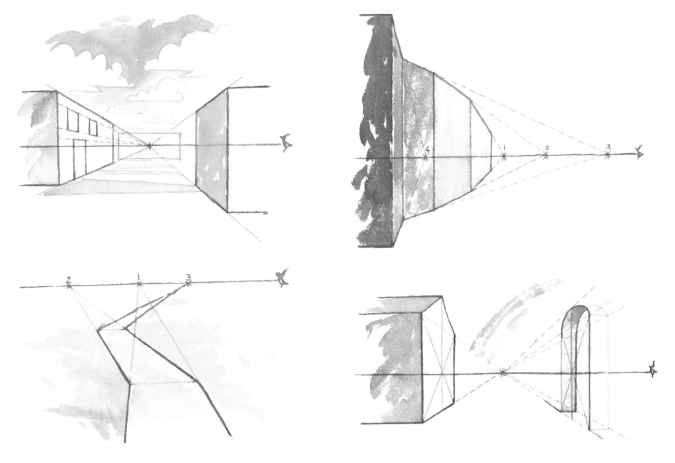

The top left diagram shows a single point, with the lines of perspective emanating from it. Note that the point can move from side to side, as in the bottom left diagram. The top right diagram has a moving vanishing point to show a zig-zagging wall. If you turn this book on its side you will notice how this could also represent a road going up and down hill.

In the bottom right diagram I have indicated how to find the centre of a wall, in order to position the eaves of a roof, and how to establish the centre for an arch.

Two-point perspective

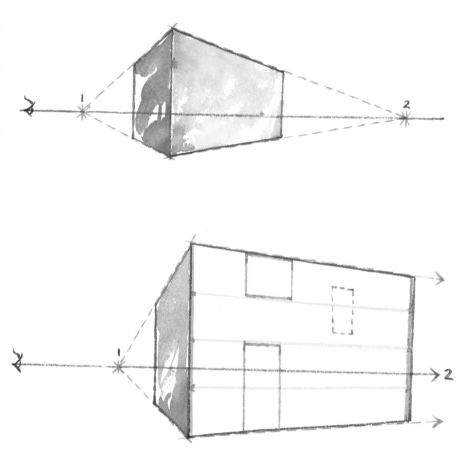

Two-point perspective does involve rather more complex issues than one-point perspective. Two-point perspective occurs when looking at the corner of a building. The lines of the walls on either side of the corner, if extended towards the horizon, appear to lead towards two points in the distance. Obviously if buildings are set at different angles to you, two-point perspective is necessary; the sides of the walls converge to two separate points on your eye-level. This can be seen in the little diagram I have drawn. However, the subject becomes more complicated when the building under scrutiny has one wall almost directly facing you; in this case the lines converge to a point miles beyond your piece of paper, and you have to imagine where this point would be. To delineate the windows and doors you may need to divide a line to the right of your piece of paper by the same number of divisions as the corner of the building. This will provide you with a grid, against which you can set the angles of your windows and doors.

Before starting a large painting, it is sensible to produce a small sketch of the scene, and to calculate where these lines are likely to converge. In this way you can iron out potential problems.

One way of establishing the angles of roof lines or ground lines is to use what I call the 'parallel pencil method'. To do this hold out a pencil or brush, parallel to your eyes. This corresponds to the horizontal plane at which you are painting your picture. Now just tilt the pencil until it reflects the angle of the roof line in front of you. Then transfer this angle to your piece of paper. Hold your sketch-book up behind the pencil, and note the

angle on it. Once this technique has been established, any angle can be arrived at by the same method. The point at which these angles converge is your eye-level, and all windows, doors, sills etc can be drawn emanating from this.

There is a device to help you understand two-point perspective. In fact it is a variation of a method used by Albrecht Dürer, who originated the idea.

You need a wooden frame 24in (60cm) by 18in (50cm) over which has been stretched a sheet of acetate. On this acetate is drawn, in ink, a grid of lines 1in (25mm) apart. Mount the frame vertically roughly

In the top diagram our eye-level is denoted by a purple line. As the block is being assessed in three-quarters view, its size will appear to diminish to a point, which in this instance is on our eye-level. We call this two-point perspective — where two planes lead away from the viewer.

In the lower diagram notice that the angles of the building are very slight. The angles of the doors and windows will eventually meet at a vanishing point way off the paper indicated by the two blue arrows. You have to sense where this point lies and then draw in the horizontal lines. Make a grid and divide the vertical lines equally, and you will find that the angle of the doorheads and windowsills will follow these converging lines.

18in (50cm) from your eyes so that you can just see the sides of the frame without moving your head. Divide your paper into a similar grid to the acetate. You are then able to look through the acetate grid and copy what you see on to your paper, square by square.

The level of expertise required to feel comfortable with two-point perspective can only be achieved through constant practice. Don't go too fast; start with relatively simple subjects until the principles have been established, and then go on

and work on more complex subjects as your confidence increases.

A good practice exercise involves a selection of cardboard boxes. Place these on a table, then sit down low, to give the impression that you are seeing the boxes rather more as buildings, and attempt to draw them. You could even add in rectangles to represent windows and doors. This simple device would give you sufficient material with which to explore the complexities of perspective which occur when viewing buildings on site.

Farm courtyard
Two-point perspective applies when looking into a corner. The walls of the buildings on the left will converge to a point beyond the corner to the right. Similarly, the walls of the building on the right will converge to a point on the left of the corner. These two points will be on the eye-level. The heads and sills of the doors and windows will also radiate from these points.

I have taken certain liberties with perspective, bending and curving many of the lines to add character to the buildings. Avoid using rulers 'to get it right'. This results in a stilted painting.

Three-point perspective

There will come a time when you want to create a greater sense of height in your paintings. In order to achieve this you will have to incorporate a form of perspective involving three points. This third point cannot be accurately plotted on your piece of paper, but will need to be 'sensed' at a point somewhere below your feet! Needless to say, once you have grasped the principles of two-point perspective, the problems inherent in three-point will be reasonably easy to solve. Broadly speaking, all the verticals you see in front of you (which under the other two types of perspective would always be parallel with the two sides of your paper) will converge to a point. This is the kind of phenomenon observed when looking down on some skyscrapers from a high window.

To help plot this, consider that any line directly in front of you would be absolutely vertical, and that lines to the right and left of you would appear slanted. The angle of slant increases towards the edges of the picture, thereby creating a sense of vertical depth.

You would probably use this kind of perspective when taking a very high eye-level, for example, at the level of the gutters of a building, or above the roof. If you place a tall cardboard box on the floor, stand nearby and look down on it, you should see the vertical lines apparently converging to a point well below the box.

Three-point perspective is not only confined to buildings, but comes into play when looking at any tall objects — such as trees, mountains and cliffs. This type of perspective creates a sense of depth, and is interesting to explore.

I have noticed that many stu-

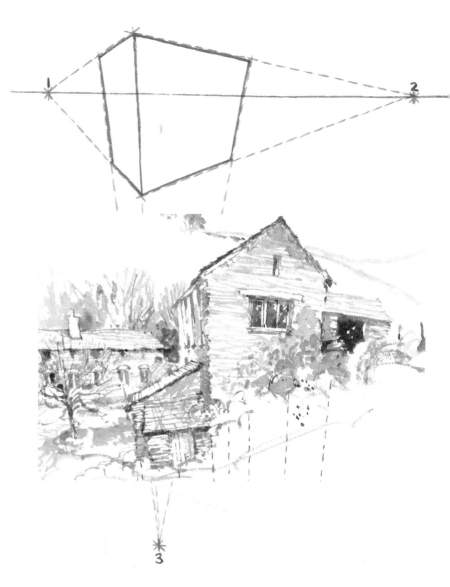

In this drawing I have demonstrated the basic principles of three-point perspective. Note that we have the same two points on the eye-level as for two-point perspective, but that well below these is a third point from which the verticals emanate. Inset into the sketch there is a small brush drawing showing how this sort of perspective can be exploited. Looking from the right to the left, the verticals are no longer parallel to the sides of the piece of paper. This gives the impression of looking down into a courtyard.

dents find it difficult to see the slanting of the vertical lines. One way is to use a frame of card that will act as your picture plane. You will notice when looking down on buildings through this frame that verticals in the building adjacent to the sides of the frame will not be parallel. By this means you will become aware of the third point perspective.

So far I have only mentioned three-point perspective when looking down on buildings and trees where the verticals radiate from a point below your feet. The same perspective also occurs when looking up. This is particularly noticeable when standing in a grove of pine trees, for example. There you will see them appear to converge at a point above your head.

Buildings seen close-up are equally subject to this appearance. When using three-point perspective try not to include too great an angle of vision or your picture will appear distorted. For a greater angle of vision another kind of perspective is required.

Poplars in France

In order to create the illusion of being above the trees, the form of three-point perspective has been used. The building to the left has more obliquely angled verticals, whereas the trees in the centre are practically vertical. For your own experimental purposes try to copy a painting similar to this; it will help you to understand how such verticals are likely to be affected.

Orbital perspective

In the explanations of the three forms of perspective, you will have noticed that all the lines have been referred to as straight ones. But is this so? If we think more logically about the way in which we see, it becomes evident that we do not look straight ahead with a fixed gaze, but that we move our heads slightly from side to side, and up and down. This enables us to see more — more than captured within the 60 degree angle of vision I mentioned earlier in this chapter. It is possible to draw what you see within an angle much greater than this — in fact, right up to 180 degrees — but none of the lines would appear straight.

Imagine that you are looking at a long wall, running directly in front of you. The ends of the wall disap-pear to the left and right. Looking to your left, you would see that the wall appears quite small from top to bottom. As you turn your head to the front and stare straight ahead, the top and the bottom of the wall appear very high, and as you swing your head further to the right the wall diminishes in height again.

To express this on paper you would have to draw two curved lines, one corresponding to the top of the wall, the other to the bottom. It may look strange, but this is in fact what happens.

I do not like straight lines very much, so a form of orbital perspec-tive helps a great deal as it enables me to bend lines, giving a greater flexibility and a more natural feel to my paintings.

You will see that not only do hori-zontal lines bow up and down but that the verticals are also affected

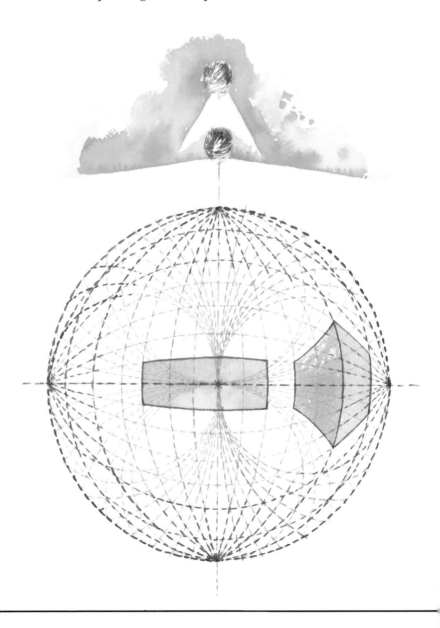

This may appear to be a rather complicated diagram, and not necessarily one that you would superimpose on your picture before starting work, but it does give some idea of the underlying grid that exists to make the orbital perspective work. You will note that all the lines curving out from the centre are in some way interconnecting to form a complete circle, ie your field of vision. You could project this on a much larger scale, and use it as a grid for plotting your picture.

The two heads positioned at the bottom of the diagram show where the angle of vision has been changed. The man at the back has an angle of vision of 60 degrees, whereas the one in front can, by moving his head, increase his field of vision to 180 degrees.

these lines appear to bow outwards from the centre. The degree of curve will increase towards the edges of your field of vision.

The fish-eye camera lens — so-called because it is thought that fish see in this way — can be used to create this effect. Even a very wide-angle lens on your camera will bend these lines as described. You can observe this by getting hold of a photograph taken with a lens of this kind; then trace over the lines and see what has been produced. A little practice at this will help you to become proficient at interpreting

this effect in the scene before you. Remember that the object of using this form of perspective is to include more in the landscape — ie cover a wider area — than would normally be possible.

This kind of perspective is very relevant to landscape painting. The curved lines of buildings relate sympathetically to those of branches in the trees, and to the natural shapes of bushes, leaves, etc, surrounding manmade forms. The curvaceous forms of clouds also relate more closely to the lines of buildings if these are slightly bent.

Farm windows
Although this picture only shows a small section of a long wall, orbital perspective has been incorporated to distort the lines, and to create the illusion of the wall coming towards you.

The other curious effect of orbital perspective is that it helps to thrust forward the point of interest. Even the tree trunk on the left has been subject to this illusion.

Making a number of small sketches like this is extremely useful in that you can build up a wider variety of subject matter for future reference.

Spiral perspective

This type of perspective is something of a personal invention. In effect it is a form of single-point perspective, but the perspective point shifts both sideways and up and down. Its main application is for pictures containing no artificial elements. For example, it can be used when painting amongst trees or undergrowth where a tunnel-like effect is required. As you can see from the accompanying diagrams it involves the principle of a spiral, where the single point emanates from the centre. The aim is to achieve a 'hole' effect with the direction of brush strokes, line of branches, grasses etc. The point at which the hole starts can be hidden, as indicated in the accompanying sketch.

An interesting characteristic of this form of spiral perspective is that by applying a kind of vortex it generates a sense of movement. There are a couple of different techniques for achieving this effect: either keep the hole very light against a darker background, as though sunshine is coming from it, or reverse this and have the hole very dark, and then allow the landscape to lighten as it emanates from it. This form of perspective tonal contrast can be exploited when looking into the undergrowth. To some extent Rembrandt used to employ this technique when implying a hidden light source.

When walking through the undergrowth, try to find some of these holes and make sketches based on this principle. Once you understand this characteristic, you will be able to untangle the apparent confusion of leaves and grasses in your work.

This sort of perspective has also been used for vignette painting, where the picture has no definite

In the top sketch we see how the single point on our eye-level rotates outward, thereby creating a spiral. This implies that the lines emanating from it occur horizontally, up and down and diagonally.

In the sketch below you can see how this spiralling then acts rather like a coiled spring, twisting and turning to create the hole effect.

rectilinear form. In other words, the outside edges of the painting have been allowed to bleed off into the white paper.

The roots for this kind of spiralling can be found in Rococo art which sought its inspiration in the natural forms of rocks and grottos. It was the way used by the Rococo artists to penetrate space and create an illusion of freedom and depth.

In order to get into this spirit you will need to look to your brush-work. I use all manner of means to generate this spiralling quality. Try wiping in a circular motion for the distant spaces, and also try soft squirrel hair brushes to produce flicks of colour that emanate from the centre of the spiral.

In evaluating a composition it is helpful to select those elements that are best able to reinforce your ideas; for example, the direction of grasses, branches, whole trees and even the sides of buildings (see the section on orbital perspective).

An obvious area where spiral perspective is noticeable is the sky. It is often with a dramatic sky that you notice how the clouds create this spiralling motion.

Fuchsia garden
This was an ideal subject for creating the 'hole' effect. I started painting with a very light pale-yellow tone spiralling out from the point at which the path disappeared. I gradually increased the colour and intensity of the plants towards the foreground to emphasise the tunnel effect.

The directions of the brush strokes are important in creating this spiral impression; note how the textures weave in and out to give this effect. I have introduced a certain amount of splattering in the foreground to imply the twists and tangles of the undergrowth.

Perspective

1 It is important to establish your eye-level at this stage, and here I have placed it about one-third up the picture. Each building is positioned at a different plane to me, and I must therefore establish the vanishing point for each plane. These are put in as very light dots on my eye-level. I then start marking in the roof lines and ground lines in a very pale blue colour. In a building of this complexity a fair amount of drawing-in is required.

2 After I have lightly sketched in all the windows, doors, chimneys etc, I start from the top and work in the main tonal areas. The wash for the sky is laid in very strongly, using a mixture of ultramarine and cerulean blue to give a dramatic effect to the clouds. The buildings are given shadow indications with a neutral grey mixed from ultramarine, a little violet and cadmium yellow.

3 The buildings are mainly white and consequently very reflective. They pick up colour from their surroundings and, in this case, from the setting sun. All the tones therefore must be very restrained. A mixture of cadmium red and ultramarine with violet has been added to give the buildings a slight 'blush', and this is subsequently washed over with a light Naples yellow. In order to make the buildings stand out, the dark greens in the background have been intensified to give contrast.

4 When painting a complicated 'buildingscape' I generally leave the ground plane until last. In this case the road goes uphill and so would have a higher vanishing point than those for the buildings.

The ground is broken up into a series of planes in order to indicate recession.

5 In the finished picture I have worked in sufficient foreground information to complete the scene, but have taken care not to make it too detailed. If the foreground is too strong, it can draw the viewer's attention away from the middle distance.

It is fun to add a touch of intrigue to a painting like this; let the road turn a corner as the horizon is approached, and leave the viewer pondering as to its ultimate destination.

CHAPTER 4

THE OUTDOOR KIT

Half the trauma of painting outdoors is deciding what on earth to take with you. Somehow all the contents of the studio, together with its creature comforts, have to be stuffed into a bag and transported to inaccessible places.

The question of what to take, or what to leave behind, can be crucial to the success of the painting. Over the years I have evolved two different types of kit depending upon the location and the circumstances in which I will be working. This chapter will give you hints on what to take and how to use it.

The lightweight sketching kit

I have evolved this collection of equipment over a long period of time. There is a variety of kits on the market, and your final choice will depend on your finances, and the sort of conditions in which you will be working.

The whole kit is designed to fit comfortably into an inside pocket of any reasonably smart jacket. If you are working out of doors, a coat pocket will, obviously, be able to contain more. However, I have often been to garden parties where this kind of portable equipment has proven invaluable.

The most important item is the box containing the paints, which should ideally include a palette for mixing. The paints can be either hard pan (as illustrated) or in tubes, but one disadvantage with the latter is that they tend to rattle around, and squeezing paint out can be time-consuming if you want to work quickly. These boxes can be made in plastic, but one of the problems I have encountered with plastic palettes is the tendency for the surface tension in the water to bubble up, making mixing rather difficult. A small amount of scrubbing powder, rubbed in to scour the surface, will prevent this.

The quality of colours in your palette is very important, and it is well worth buying the best. With inferior makes you will spend too much time trying to scrub up enough colour to do your work. Some manufacturers include a moisturiser in their paints to keep them damp, and this has its advantages.

The point of the brush should be protected by a cap. Certain brushes have been manufactured which are small enough to fit into these pocket-size palettes, but you can always saw down a standard watercolour brush. Some palettes have a thumb loop underneath to facilitate holding. Transporting water is always a problem; I use a small hip flask, and transfer the contents to a collapsible-type water pot on site. All this can be fitted into a pocket.

Finally, the paper needs to be contained in a sketch-book. I always prefer to use a spiral-type sketchbook so that I can to tear out the pages easily. The paper should be of good quality, preferably in the region of 90lb (190gsm) to 140lb (300gsm) weight. It should be reasonably hard to restrict the degree of warp whilst working.

As can be seen from the photograph this type of kit is extremely compact. Even so, the palette is large enough to allow you to produce a good range of watercolours.

The sketch-book is small so that large washes are not necessary. The brush is a No 3 sable, which is full enough to cover the page and at the same time can produce adequate detail. The colours are of good quality and are Italian, manufactured by Mamieri.

The water pot is made of corrugated plastic which collapses when not in use.

Opposite
These sketches are deliberately kept very small, and are simply used to note the basic details of a particular view: composition, colour and mood. By building on these small sketches, complete paintings can be undertaken later in the studio. I believe they have far more value than a photograph.

The large painting kit

I generally do 90 per cent of my painting outdoors. I also tend to work quite large, and the usual paper size is 22in (560mm) by 30in (760mm). I have designed a special kit which enables me to transport the equipment necessary to paint this size of picture comfortably.

The first consideration is the easel, and because I work standing up this has to be designed in such a way that the picture can be tilted just off the horizontal. I use a lightweight wooden easel because the metal ones are too heavy. This easel has been customised and has a large, specially designed piece of thin plywood bolted to it. The plywood has had three holes cut out of it — two for palettes, and one to hold a large water container. In windy weather you will need to secure the easel by means of a piece of string attached to the centre of it, and anchored by your foot or a suitable heavy rock.

Everything folds up so that I can carry it easily. Four large bulldog clips hold a container of paper which is surrounded by polythene and this keeps the paintings dry. I have a waterproof bag containing all my paint tubes and brushes, rolled up in a protective material, and soft tissue paper for mopping up.

My water container needs to be quite large, and it actually carries approximately a gallon (5 litres) of water. This is the only heavy item in my kit, but it is essential; I need to use a lot of clean water in order to keep my colours clear.

As a luxury I take along a lightweight folding angler's-style stool. On cold days, I include in my kit a thermos of hot drink — a touch of comfort in inclement conditions!

The whole package is designed to be carried by one person, otherwise I would be confined to locations close to the car.

Remember, when working large, that the paper must be well secured. In the past I used masking tape but have since discovered that large bulldog clips are more efficient as they enable me to stretch the paper as I work. For this reason the board size is related to the paper size.

You will find that attention to detail and portability when deciding on what to take will reward you with some fine experiences in landscape painting.

Here we see the whole kit laid out ready for use. The plywood panel has been designed to hold two square palettes with deep pans which give many options for mixing. There is a hole in the centre of the plywood which takes the plastic water container. The paper is kept in a polythene sleeve, attached to the ply with bulldog clips. The brushes are kept in a split bamboo wrap for safety. On the ground is a waterproof shoulder-bag which holds all the accessories — paints, brushes, palettes and water container. The folding stool is from a fishing-tackle shop, and the thermos flask is for my refreshment. The whole kit folds down and can be carried by one person.

Painting out of doors, with a large piece of paper, can be somewhat problematical. It is essential that your paper is firmly fixed to the plywood, hence the large bulldog clips. These clips also enable you to stretch the paper whilst working.

The type of painting you produce depends upon the weather. In muggy conditions, when there is a lot of moisture in the atmosphere, washes take quite a time to dry, and so doing a series of these can be most frustrating. In these circumstances I adopt a different technique, involving white lines and spaces between colours, which obviously speeds up the drying time. On a hot sunny day washes can easily be laid one over the other.

When working large you need to be able to get back from the picture to assess its overall unity, and for this reason I work standing up. The stool is really for relaxation time whilst the paint dries. Painting in an upright position also enables you to work freely over the whole surface without being too niggardly.

Paper

I use a variety of paper types. Each one has different characteristics, relating to texture, absorbency and weight.

Watercolour paper is available in three different types, and the texture of each depends on how it has been pressed during manufacture.

The first type is hot pressed (known as 'HP'). It has a slightly glazed surface, the result of being passed between steel sheets. This surface is ideal for detail work, but too smooth for fine graded washes.

The second texture is called a 'Not' surface. This 'Not' refers to the fact that it is not hot pressed, and therefore has a light texturing.

The third surface is known as 'rough', and its texture is adequately described by this term. This type of paper has only been pressed once during manufacture. It is used for very broad brush methods of painting, where a lot of sparkle and texture is required.

The paper most generally used by the watercolourist is the Not finish. This surface can vary considerably in terms of the fineness of texture. The degree of absorbency is important in a paper.

Some manufacturers add a mixture of glycerine and/or starch to their papers, which helps to make

Fabriano 90lb (190gsm) HP
This Italian paper has a smooth, fine texture. It is relatively absorbent, and enables one to experiment with detail. Washes will have a slight blooming effect on this paper.

Saunders RWS 140lb (300gsm) Not
This is a classic type of watercolour paper, made in England, which displays all the characteristics of a good Not surface. The texture is intermediate with good random qualities. It is reasonably hard and is ideally suited to beginners as well as professionals. You can erase easily by blotting out or sponging. This robust paper stands up well to severe handling with knife blades etc.

them more absorbent.

When working outdoors in muggy conditions it is important to use a paper that has been treated in this way, as a hard paper would take longer to dry; the washes would 'sit' on the surface.

The third relevant factor when choosing paper is its weight. This is often referred to in pounds per ream (470–500 sheets) or grammes per square metre (gsm). The average lightweight paper is approximately 90lb (190gsm), and the type I nor-mally use is 140lb (300gsm). The weight of the paper governs how much it is likely to move when washes have been applied to it. The greater the weight, the more stable it is. When working small, a lightweight paper is perfectly ade-quate, but a larger painting requires a heavier weight paper.

There may be times when you want to add some opacity to your painting, by the introduction of an opaque Naples yellow or white. To help with this there are a variety of tinted papers which are available, varying in colour from cool, grey tints to warm, brown ones.

The kind of paper you choose is very much a question of personal taste. If you work quickly, a more absorbent surface is preferable. Those of you who work smaller, with much finer detail, should select a smoother texture. Many manufac-turers will supply samples for you to choose from; take advantage of this, and experiment until you find a paper that suits you.

Barcham Green De Wint 90lb (190gsm) Rough
This is an example of a rough textured paper which also incorporates a tint. This allows opaque paints to show up and gives your pictures an extra dimension. It is ideally suited to textural experiments but will not necessarily give much satisfaction to the detail painter.

Moulin De Gue 140lb (300gsm) Not
This is one of my favourite absorbent types of paper, which is actually an etching paper made in France. It is perfect for rapid working, and is ideal when the atmosphere is damp. It does not take kindly to a lot of rubbing out as the paper lifts very easily, but it is excellent for direct brush work.

Tools

The kind of tools you use in water-colour painting are of paramount importance. I cannot stress too strongly how vital it is to choose the best quality brushes available; one good brush is worth twenty inferior ones. Brushes are something of a personal fetish. I am fascinated by their shapes, qualities and the way they work.

As you can see from the accompanying photograph, there is a vast variety of brushes to choose from, differing in hair type, in length and in shape. The most important, and the one used by watercolourists throughout the world, is the sable hair brush. It is naturally very springy and resilient, and beautifully versatile. It draws to an extremely fine point almost invisible to the naked eye, and you can use it for almost anything from broad washes to fine detail. Sable brushes vary both in size and shape. The size is related to a numbering system from 00 to 12: the larger the number, the larger the size. There will be occasions when you may need a softer brush stroke, and for this a fine squirrel is highly suitable. These brush types are ideal for painting leaves of different sizes and forms and for laying small areas of wash.

Sable and squirrel brushes both come in various shapes. The round or pencil, as it is often referred to on the continent, is ideal for general work, detail and washes. Flat brushes, ideal for painting buildings or angled corners, are identified by the flattened ferrule (the metal part of the brush), which gives them a square-cut chisel-like appearance. The third shape is the filbert which also has a flattened ferrule, but in this case the hairs are either rounded or pointed at the top. These filberts are ideal for tree shapes in the distance and for leaf shapes in the foreground, and can also be used on edge to produce lines, ie branches etc. All the above brushes are manufactured in the West, and have been evolved over many years.

I generally advise beginners to select a No 5 or No 6 round sable. This brush is very versatile and will start off the collection which can be

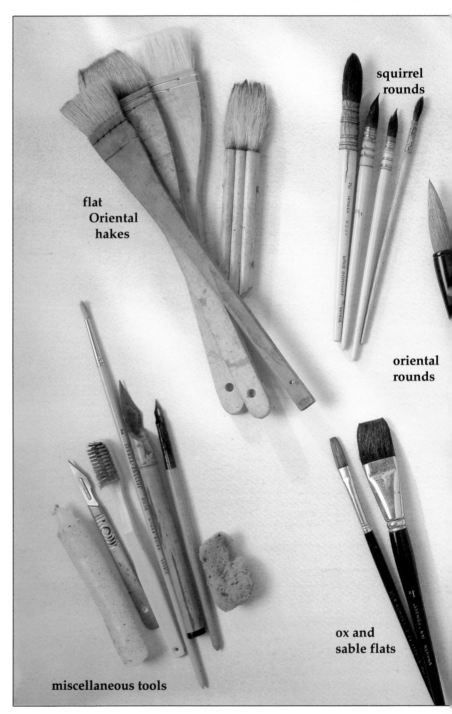

squirrel
rounds

flat
Oriental
hakes

oriental
rounds

ox and
sable flats

miscellaneous tools

augmented as work progresses.

There is a separate group of brushes that has originated in the Orient, and these have quite different characteristics to their Western counterparts. They are made of a softer hair and are used vertically. Several have a stiff 'drawing-in' hair in the centre of the brush, with soft outer layers which act as a water reservoir. These brushes are very versatile, and many different types of stroke can be obtained.

Another kind of Oriental brush is the hake, which is similar to our Western flat. This is a very soft lightweight brush which has many similar characteristics to the flat. Depending upon the angle in which it is held, it can produce both broad washes and straight lines.

When I am working standing up, I need to be well away from the paper surface, particularly towards the end of a painting when the final details have to be added to tie the picture together. The watercolourist's brush is usually very short, and so at this stage I use special long-handled brushes. This allows me to work well away from the painting, so that I can judge the unifying effect of the final details.

When adding detail like fine branches, grasses or the rigging on boats, I use a special brush called a rigger. This is designed for this particular purpose, and has long hair (usually sable) drawn to a fine tip.

In every watercolourist's kit there are miscellaneous tools which help to add variety to the texture of a painting. The most important is a soft sponge for wiping out areas or for softly blending colours.

Second to this will be a group of pens, some manufactured from bamboo, which can draw in watercolour with a fairly broad line. For fine line work a steel mapping-style pen is also very useful.

There are occasions when you might want to scratch out fine white lines, or create white textures on your painting. For this a scalpel or something similar is ideal.

To complete the kit I always have a roll of soft tissue and some cloth for blotting surplus paint.

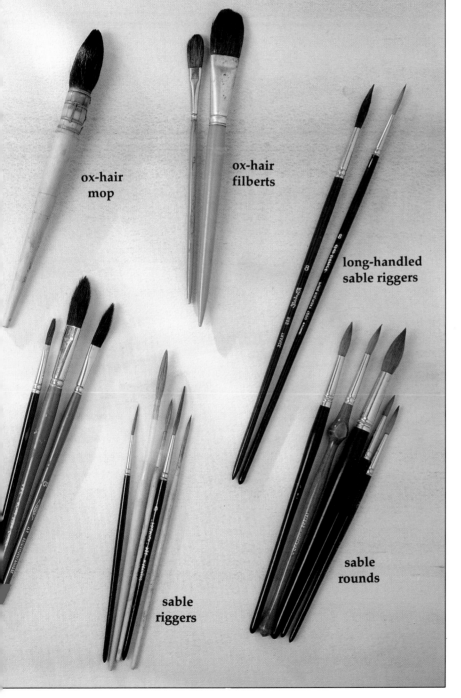

ox-hair mop

ox-hair filberts

long-handled sable riggers

sable riggers

sable rounds

Paints and colour

There are two important points to consider when buying paints. Firstly, the nature and characteristics of the pigment itself, and secondly the actual colour.

Different manufacturers use a variety of pigments in making up specific colours. So when buying a particular colour, check that if it is not made by your normal manufacturer, it really is the one you want. The pigments themselves are ground with a medium, usually gum arabic, but a gum traganth is used for some of the heavier types. This also helps to improve the plasticity of the paint. The gum is instrumental in attaching the particles of pigment to the paper. Formaldehyde (a preservative) can be added to those pigments containing gum, to prevent the growth of mould. Because of its hydrophillic properties, glycerine is usually added to some pan colours, and this helps to keep these paints slightly moist for ease of working. Wetting agents, such as ox-gall, are added to some paints to improve flow, and to allow fine dispersal for wet-into-wet areas.

Manufacturers are generally extremely careful in the preparation of their products. Among the best of these, and the ones I use are Winsor & Newton of England, Schmincke of West Germany, Maimeri of Italy and Lefranc & Bourgeois of France.

Pigments are made up of various substances such as earths, metallic salts and plant roots. As a result, some pigments may precipitate. This results in a grainy appearance in some washes, especially when using ultramarine, raw umber, some cerulean blues and manganese blue.

Paint manufacturers cannot produce an absolute primary colour, ie red, yellow or blue. The colours they make will inevitably be either warm

Primary colours

The full range of the three primary colours is shown, from full intensity, through the addition of water, to finest, lightest tones.

The pigments themselves vary in tone from dark through to light. The nature of the colour also changes from yellow/blue to red/blue, yellow/red through to blue/red, and from green/yellow through to red/yellow.

Explore the various hues produced by different manufacturers.

Secondary colours

These comprise the violets, greens and oranges. I use only one orange — a cadmium orange. There is a variety of greens available, from quite cold blue greens through to earthy, warm greens.

The violets generally cannot be mixed with any degree of intensity. Here is a range of mauves through to dark violet which is useful for darkening reds and also for giving warmth in skies.

Tertiary colours

These tertiary colours, ie browns, are generally made up from earth colours. The umber and sienna have a raw and burnt option, the latter being the warmer of the two. These colours are very useful for creating neutral tones.

The colour wheel
In this colour wheel you will note that opposite each primary colour is a secondary — its complementary. Red is opposite the green, yellow is opposite the violet and blue opposite the orange. In order to create neutral complementaries, adding a touch of red to the green, or vice versa, will make the opposite appear more vibrant. Note also that as you go round the wheel one colour merges gradually into another, ie the red going through orange to yellow, then to pale green, then to blue.

Careful control of colour mixing maintains clarity and keeps the painting vibrant.

to hot (red) or cool to cold (blue). For example alizarin is a cold red which, because of the blue in it, appears slightly mauve in colour. Ultramarine blue is a warm blue; because of its red content, it appears slightly violet.

Secondary colours, which are an admixture of two of the primary colours, can vary according to whether these primaries are hot or cold. A warm green is comprised of a yellow with red in it, and blue with a touch of red in it. Thus, if you mix cadmium yellow (which contains a touch of red) with any blue, you will produce a warm green. If you mix lemon yellow (containing blue), with cerulean blue (which has yellow in it), you will produce a light, cool green.

Tertiary colours are an admixture of three of the primaries and give rise to a range of neutral colours or browns. These will vary according to the amounts of red, yellow or

blue that have been mixed together. Paint manufacturers provide a range of tertiary colours made from various earths.

I never use black, preferring to mix a very dark colour, say, a combination of phthalo dark blue with an alizarin crimson. Mixing these two dark primaries together has a 'cancelling-out' effect, and results in either a warm or cold black.

Your landscape paintings will be brought to life when you learn to exploit one of the phenomena of the colour spectrum — that of complementary colours. Owing to the way in which we receive colour in our eyes, certain ones have a complementary effect when used together. For example, red is complementary to green. Therefore, when painting a predominantly green landscape, the use of small patches of red, in the branches of trees etc, will help to enliven the painting. The colour-wheel diagram explains which hues

are complementary.

It is often a good idea to reduce one of the complementary colours to a neutral, by adding the two colours together. For example, a touch of yellow in a violet will produce a more grey violet, and this will enhance any yellow shades nearby.

Looking for and using complementary colours in your landscape painting will bring freshness and vibrancy to your work.

A very important point to bear in mind when mixing paints is to keep your colours, and therefore your palette, clean. Muddy paint will always occur when you have three or more colours together, or when you layer colours on your painting. Two or three layers are the maximum you should apply.

If this ever happens to your painting rinse it under the tap. This will take off the surplus colour and refresh the paper surface. When dry you can recommence.

Tools control

Good brush control is the key to success, and it is therefore important to develop your own individual touch when handling the brush. Specific sections in a painting require particular brushes. It is pointless to use a fine sable when laying a wash, or to attempt any detail with a brush too large and without a good point.

The way in which you hold the brush determines the fluidity of your stroke. Many people tend to grip it far too tightly, as if holding a writing pen. The brush should be held just off the vertical, with the little finger distancing the tip from the surface of the paper.

Your whole body should, ideally, be free and unrestricted, so that every stroke is flexible. Certain techniques may need to be practised on

a separate piece of paper to ensure that when you start painting you can execute the strokes with confidence. This method of preparation can be likened to the way in which a violinist practises to produce a spontaneous quality in his music.

You should remember also that the brush has two aspects — the tip and the body — and that strokes are worked quite frequently from the tip to the body, and back to the tip again, to produce specific marks. Dragging the brush sideways, spreading the hairs delicately over the surface of the paper, produces marks which reflect the texture and absorbency of the paper. When laying a wash, over either a small or a large area, make sure that the brush is well loaded with paint, and that the board is tilted at a slight angle

towards you. This allows the paint to flow downwards evenly when applied horizontally.

In detail work, however, you need rather less paint. The brush should be drawn to a fine tip, and you can use soft tissue to wipe off the excess. The strokes are then applied, taking into account the quality and nature of the brush tip.

Dry brush work, as the name implies, is the technique when very little paint is put on the brush; it is then dragged over the surface of the paper, just hitting the peaks of the texture. This leaves white spaces or light areas in your work, which provide sparkle and interest.

To achieve very fine line work, for example the branches of trees, etc the rigger is employed, and used in a trailing motion. The brush needs

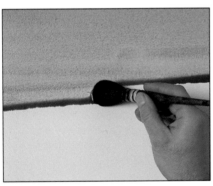

Wash

Side of the brush

Fine lines with a rigger

Highlighting with a scalpel

Wiping with a sponge

Ribbon stroke with a hake

to be well filled, with just the tip drawn to a point.

Instead of using white paint in your watercolours, highlights can be produced by using a scalpel or sharp knife if the paint is already dry. Alternatively, while the paint is still wet, you can scratch the surface of the paper with your fingernail or some suitable tool. Light areas can be blotted out by using soft tissue or bits of cotton wool. Once the painting is dry, light areas or even subtle merging can be produced by wiping the surface gently with a soft, natural sponge. A sponge can also be used to blend colours together when you want to produce a sensation of depth in the far distance.

Splattering paint with a tooth-brush or a hog's hair sable can be effective when you want to indicate a varied textural surface, such as leaves in the distance, or pebbles on the beach. Control the area covered by using your hand as a mask, or by putting pieces of scrap paper over those parts you wish to protect. Overuse of these techniques can make a painting look a bit con-trived, so use them with discretion.

The flat brush is used for produc-ing broad strokes, like decorating a door, but it also produces ribbon-like strokes and straight lines. The hake is very versatile in this respect.

In the early days of watercolour painting, many small pictures were almost entirely produced by a form of stippling. Small dabs of paint of closely regulated tones were woven over the entire surface of the pic-ture. This gave a mosaic-like quality to the finished painting, and stip-pling part of your work can convey this fine detail quality.

One of the common pitfalls of watercolour painting is learning how to gauge the drying time. It is no good attempting any detail in a painting if the underlying work is not yet dry. For crisp, defined details you need to work on a com-pletely dry surface. In the studio you can, of course, use a hairdrier.

The amount of bleed is also affect-ed by this factor, and some bleed is essential in order to create depth. Determining how wet or dry you should work is a question of prac-tice and experience.

These techniques are the vocabu-lary of your painting. To broaden this store of knowledge, analyse other painters' pictures and, where possible, watch them at work.

Tip to body stroke

Detail with a pen

Dry brush work

Splattering with a toothbrush

Blotting with a soft tissue

Stippling

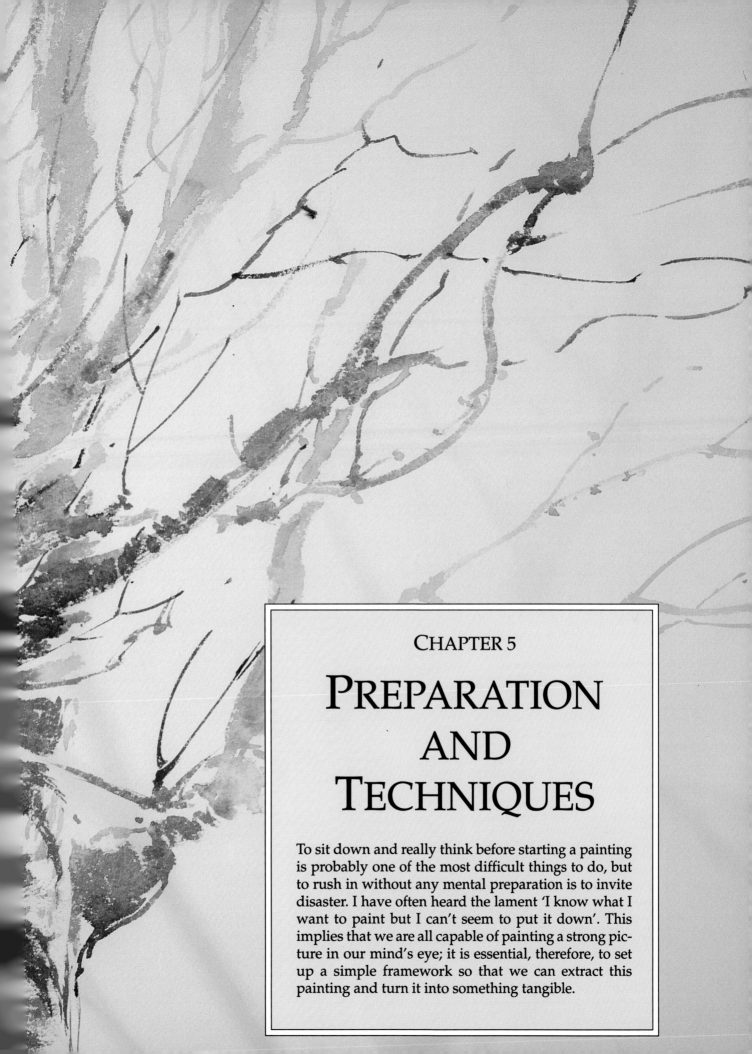

CHAPTER 5

PREPARATION AND TECHNIQUES

To sit down and really think before starting a painting is probably one of the most difficult things to do, but to rush in without any mental preparation is to invite disaster. I have often heard the lament 'I know what I want to paint but I can't seem to put it down'. This implies that we are all capable of painting a strong picture in our mind's eye; it is essential, therefore, to set up a simple framework so that we can extract this painting and turn it into something tangible.

Drawing-in

Drawing-in

It is inevitable that the first strokes in a painting will be rather tentative. Putting down light marks to indicate the approximate positions of the salient parts in your picture requires a form of drawing-in. Use a flexible brush at this stage so that the mind can wander freely over the picture plane. A pencil should be avoided, as it might mark the surface of the paper and result in a messy finish. In the event of your drawing-in lines being in the wrong place, they can be erased easily with a little water and a light sponging.

Do not let your drawing become too tight at this point, or it will be difficult to make alterations later. To maintain your interest, and to keep the work lively, experiment with different colours pertinent to the objects you are painting — pale blues for horizons, pale greens and yellows for trees.

Negative spaces

In watercolour painting the natural progression is to work from light colours through to dark. Sometimes you may overwork the dark areas by applying successive layers of paint, and so it is a good idea to establish some of these darker tones early, in order to keep them fresh. You must be acutely conscious of the light sections in your painting, and be able to leave these behind as positive shapes. A classic example is the treatment of clouds. In order to show white clouds you need to paint the blue of the sky behind them, and this can be done when the paper is either dry or damp. To soften the edges of the clouds in dry work, all you need to do is wipe gently with water, and then sponge it off.

Negative painting is also used where light tree trunks show up against dark foliage. You must identify the shapes of the foliage between the branches, and paint these accordingly.

Drawing in lumps

There may be times when you will not want to laboriously draw-in your line work, and then fill in with colour. The following system will speed up your work, and help you to see the negative shapes more positively.

I describe this system as 'drawing in lumps'. It means identifying the shadow areas of an object, rather like a polarised photograph where all the greys have been taken away, and you are left with a simple black-and-white image. These shadow areas may include not only the object itself, but also the shadows it casts, and the way it links adjacent objects.

Painting in this way necessitates seeing the mid-tone colour of the area. This can range from being quite light to very dark. I use a versatile Oriental brush for this work; the brush you select needs a large body which comes to a fine tip.

In painting the boat in the picture here I have seen the bulk of the hull as a single tone, and I have left white areas to denote reflections from the water. This is a form of polarised painting that is closely linked to observing the negative spaces.

Autumn foliage

1 Foliage in the foregound is very much like a jigsaw puzzle. You must accept that numerous dabs of colour will be required to portray the intricacies of tone and colour observed in natural vegetation.

The drawing must be very simple. I start with a very pale cadmium yellow mixed with a little cadmium orange to indicate the basic leaf structures. I am using an Oriental brush; by pressing it down from the tip to the body, leaf shapes are produced. You need to see the way in which the yellows form clusters. Try to express the different tones to be found in the groups of leaves in the distance, and the single ones in the foreground.

2 Because the branches lie both in front of and behind the leaves, you need to indicate their positions at this stage. The lines of branches vary both in colour and intensity from bottom to top. You must leave spaces behind the boughs, so that the foliage looks as if it is growing towards the viewer, and for this I use a rigger brush.

Notice how the branches cross over one another and bifurcate at neat junctions; if they did not, this section could look haphazard. Some speed and dexterity is needed at this stage to keep the work lively.

3 Some of the branches are much broader than others, and here I am using the same Oriental brush as for the leaves to scrape the paint sideways, giving a broken quality to the branch forms. Notice how I have had to stop and start to portray the leaves that overlap the branch and, at the same time, have allowed some of the paint to bleed into the leaves to give depth to the painting.

4 The painting is now becoming more complex. I am inserting the foliage behind the branches, leaving a lot of the light leaf spaces behind. This is where fitting the jigsaw puzzle together takes place. To achieve this successfully you must wait for the paint to dry before going on to the next stage.

5 The final dark accents are now added. In the bottom left-hand corner branches have appeared as a result of painting in the dark areas behind. At this stage I lay on the branches that cross over some of the foliage, thereby drawing attention to the vegetation which is coming towards the viewer.

Shadows on branches are best described by painting across the vertical line, rather than up and down. This helps to create more tension in the line of the branch.

Walls

1 Portraying a wall successfully is largely a matter of getting the texture right, and this is best achieved by laying several layers of paint to build up the final effect.

I start off by applying a multi-coloured wash to indicate the mortar that would exist between the stones and bricks. I use a well loaded brush, applied horizontally, and add subtle variations to the colour as I go.

2 In this demonstration I draw in the roof line and the window. The stonework here is random, and variations in colour from blue/greys to warm greys are applied in complete stone shapes, leaving behind the mortar joints as white spaces. Care must be taken in arranging these colour areas to simulate what in fact occurs.

The side of the brush is then used to indicate brickwork, again subtly varying the colours so as to produce the textural variations that are found in old brick.

3 Attention is now given to the window. The basic timber colour is applied, and then very dark shadows are added to indicate reflections in the glass. This needs to be done crisply to make it look realistic.

4 The roof is given an initial pale wash of ultramarine and cerulean blue. The slight graininess of ultramarine will add texture to the slates.

The line work is put in freely, with rather jerky strokes, to indicate the break up of the edge of the slates. Perspective is implied by the vertical lines to help the roof 'lie down'. The colour of the line work and its tone must be adjusted as the slates come towards you.

5 This is when we need to introduce the variety of textures in the stonework, brickwork and woodwork.

Secondary tones are introduced to the stonework, concentrating on the lower sections of each stone, and then on the underside of the brickwork. I just add a slightly stronger blue to the original mix for the stonework and deepen the red for the brickwork, rather than use black. Then the toothbrush is used to give some flecks of colour — reds on the bricks, and violet-greys amongst the stones. This must be controlled so as not to go over the window section. Shadows from trees near the wall can be added here once the splattering has dried. Use a sponge or soft tissue to blot up any stray areas.

6 The final touches involve the use of a scalpel to scrape out highlights on the stonework and the roof area. This can be done either with the flat of the blade to make the colour a little paler, or with the point to scratch deeply and pick out highlights and line work.

Taking a small area like this wall and exploring it in depth is very illuminating for the watercolourist.

Sky

1 This is a classic example of negative painting. No drawing-in is required, as to put lines around clouds would detract from their illusive quality.

I commence by laying in the blue sky behind the clouds, using a mixture of cerulean blue and ultramarine. This colour tends to dry rather lighter than one would expect so can be put in reasonably dark. I have to be aware of the shapes of the clouds as I progress downwards, building the colour up across the paper as I go.

2 As the clouds diminish in the distance I introduce a subtle variation in the sky colour behind. This time I use almost pure cerulean, graduating to a touch of violet. This work is done quite rapidly.

3 In order to show the variety of the clouds I have introduced colour changes — some cadmium yellow, and cadmium red with the violet — to create the feeling of the sun lying low on the horizon. These strokes must be kept horizontal to give depth.

4 I continue applying these horizontal strokes, gradually merging them into pale blue to indicate the sea. These lines then slowly widen and thicken to create the illusion of the water coming towards the viewer. This work is done quickly to keep the edges wet, and I can soften these with blotting or by using the sponge.

5 I am now introducing the shadow areas in the clouds, using a touch of violet, ultramarine and raw umber to give warmth. It is important to understand how these shadows work. I am implying here that the sun is positioned just above right centre, which means that it lights up both sides of the cloud intersecting the top of the picture. However, only the upper edges of the clouds to the left and right catch the sunlight.

6 Final softening and pulling together of the various cloud forms are accomplished with the use of a sponge. All the negative shapes have now unified and the illusion of a warm, cloudy sky is achieved.

Foregrounds

Beach

It is generally wise to keep most foregrounds simple. In this case I have attempted to show the perspective of the beach by using radiating lines, with the vanishing point in front of me. Tonal planes have been introduced to create depth. Finally texture detail has been added, with the dabs of paint becoming smaller and finer as the beach recedes. This creates the illusion of distance. This example shows how a very flat plane can be achieved.

Foliage

Dense foliage is, by its very nature, quite complex. When such complicated areas occur in the foreground, don't fall into the trap of trying to portray them too precisely; treat them in broad abstract patterns, saving the main interest for the middle distance.

Water

Again, it is important to keep this section simple. You can use ripples and wave formations to lead the viewer's eye from the edge of the painting in towards the main centre of interest. Do not make your contrasting tones too dark, or you might draw the eye away at the expense of the main focal attraction.

Dittisham pier

In this painting my foreground consists of both water and beach, and you can see that in relative terms to the whole picture it is kept simple. Many students have trouble with the foreground, usually because they do not understand its real purpose. The main requirement is that the foreground should lead the eye into the scene. Certain parts of it will intersect the edge of the picture, and these areas can be used to direct the eye. For example, where the beach joins the water, certain definite ripple shapes

intersect the left of the painting. All colour gradations in this region need to be kept fairly soft, with maybe the odd stress in the tones to provide muted interest. In this instance I wanted the foreground to reflect something of the nature of the sky, which is a mackerel sky with flecks of warm yellow light. In the water the character of these lights changes subtly and my strokes become crisper and straighter. This gives the impression of a slight oiliness in the movement of the water.

Opaque painting

1 Working on tinted paper enables you to introduce an opacity to your work. The use of white (either Chinese white or designer's gouache, which is pigment mixed with a little china clay) or Naples yellow should be restrained so as not to destroy the transparent nature of watercolour. Here I am using a large Oriental brush to block in the sky and to introduce small touches of white to indicate the light on top of the clouds.

2 The subject is a stormy beach near to my home.

The cliffside has been put in with sideways strokes of the brush, using a rich mixture of ultramarine, raw umber, cadmium orange and burnt sienna. I have used a small squirrel-hair brush. The sea is blocked in with basic mid-tones. In order to create a feeling of movement here I sat and watched the water for quite a while, trying to understand the basic make-up of the waves. The lower tones are then added, which help to bind some of the dark areas together, and I introduce Naples yellow into the sand, and white to create the foam in the crashing waves.

3 This painting was done on a windy, blustery day, and I secured the easel by means of a loop of string attached to my foot. To create the effect of wind I had to indicate a strong 'left to right' motion in the painting, with the clouds sweeping diagonally towards the land, and the sea moving horizontally in towards the beach. Keeping this sense of movement in the front of your mind will help to direct the brush strokes, and the consequent result.

4 The painting is mainly about the water, and therefore the tonal detail of the trees and the land was kept to a minimum. To produce the impression of light behind the headland, shadows from the orange section of trees to the right were painted in, using a burnt sienna mixed with a little raw umber. The colours in this painting are mainly earth ones, with the exception of the cerulean blue and the opaque white and Naples yellow. So long as you wrap up warmly, painting in these conditions can be very exhilarating.

CHAPTER 6

CREATING ATMOSPHERE

There comes a stage in your development when you will be able to paint a scene competently, as you visualise it. But is this enough? The artist is always looking for something new — a special something which will give his work life. It is frequently referred to as atmosphere.

To accomplish atmosphere you must be very sensitive to the scene before you, and one way of developing this instinct is to paint the same view several times. This should not be boring, as all the subtle variations in the landscape will become manifest the more you explore a particular view.

Atmospheric variations I

Above This is a picture of a very beautiful river near my home, and I have painted this scene many times without fear of repeating myself. The atmosphere and lighting change so frequently that one can enjoy a constant source of inspiration. This example shows the soft lighting experienced in early morning on a summer's day.

All the following studies provide an opportunity to explore what happens to a landscape when varied light conditions create different atmospheres. You can only understand the landscape and its moods by in-depth study of this kind.

Opposite above Again early morning, but this time somewhat later in the year, at low tide. The light is coming from behind the trees, and creates sombre silhouettes. The whole picture is suffused with the same cool, yellow light.

Opposite below On this occasion the tide is in; it is an afternoon in late spring, with the light cast onto the trees. The greens are very fresh and pale, with that slight mistiness that occurs when water starts to evaporate.

Atmospheric variations II

Above Here the lighting is distinctly autumnal. The river is relatively calm, with striations or planes indicating the ripples and giving a soft, languid air. The trees again are shown in very simple silhouette form, with masts and sails treated by negative painting. No white paint is used in this picture.

Opposite above Summer produces bright greens when the sun is high. This can sometimes be rather harsh, so I have explored the activity that occurs on the river at this time of year by using the interest and colours of the boats to provide movement and focus.

Opposite below This is a semi-overcast day where all the colour has become grey and would, under normal circumstances, appear a little dull. I have introduced violets and pink in order to create a rather sombre atmosphere. Small areas of interest — the birds in the distance, for example — have been obtained by scratching-out to reveal the white paper. I have employed a steel pen, dipped into the watercolour, to highlight details, and to draw the eye to the boats in the distance.

Foliage colour rhythms

When confronted with a mass of foliage, a seemingly endless sea of green, the painter is often bewildered and believes that every single leaf must be accounted for — an impossible task! When the problem is analysed, however, a number of separate elements are revealed.

First of all, there are different tones of green, ranging from dark hues in the shadows to twinkling lights where leaves turn to the sun.

Secondly, there are endless variations in the hues of green — warm orange green, or cool lemon green, for example — such a huge range that it becomes very exciting.

Thirdly, you must consider the shapes in front of you. You will notice that trees vary from rounded to fan-shaped, elongated to ragged. These forms interlock to provide a random patchwork quilt of greens.

Fourthly, look even more intently and you will see that the textural qualities vary — fine, feathery detail in the distance becomes pointillist in the middle distance, with defined leaf shapes in the foreground. These textures vary with different leaf shapes. Oak, aspen, willow and sycamore add their rich touches to break up the monotony of green.

Finally, there are the almost musical rhythms of the foliage. Wind and sun conspire to change its direction and movement, giving the painter the opportunity to place touches of colour that weave in various directions to indicate motion.

These five ways of analysing our 'impenetrable' greenery are the first stages towards seeing the order in nature. You can experiment with the various techniques that have been evolved for depicting foliage. Your brushes are the tools which produce the variety of strokes necessary to indicate different leaf types. For example, small touches can be executed on a light-green ground by using the tip of a small sable. A slightly larger sable, dragged sideways with rather dry paint, will imply feathery foliage. Alternatively, a flat brush like the hake can produce the softer fan-like forms of a tree in the distance. Using a specific brush for a leaf or tree form demands deft and delicate handling. Discovering and selecting the right brush is part of the joy in watercolour painting.

The texture of foliage often requires a certain unstructured approach that might not be possible with conventional brush handling.

One of these, for example, is sponging. Sponges come in different types, from fine-grained to coarse, and vary from manmade (with very circular holes) to the more random hole structure of the natural sponge. The way to use a sponge is to first lay down some basic washes, wet-into-wet. When these have almost dried, dab the sponge into concentrated colour on your palette, and apply it lightly to your painting. Where the underpainting is slightly damp, the foliage texture will be softly merged to create depth. When all under-

Swinging tree
This splendid tree, in a friend's garden, is used by the local children, who swing from it on a long rope. I have used it as an opportunity for exploring colours other than green. Note that the trees on the horizon are in fact a cool red with orange. The large tree itself is an intermingling of practically every colour on my palette. I have deliberately radiated all the colours from the centre in a spiral motion which is reminiscent of the children swinging below. Exploring the movement and colour in this way helps to create a different kind of energy in your painting.

painting is dry, continued application of the sponge will produce more defined areas which will bring the foliage 'forward' towards the viewer. It is important to subtly alter the nature of the green used, or the effect will be dull and rather monotonous.

Another technique rather similar to sponging is that of ragging. Rags of various types can be used, from cotton to muslin, though very heavy cloths with a pronounced texture, like corduroy, are not suitable. Screwed-up paper is also useful; it can be used effectively to provide dark tones, to indicate shadow areas in trees, for example. Occasionally you might need to show billions of little leaves, which would be inordinately time-consuming if painted with a brush. These can be indicated with a little splattering of the paint, either using a stiff toothbrush or an

oil-painter's hog's-hair brush. I find the latter most useful when directing the paint into small areas. Again, ensure you vary the greens to keep the painting lively and exciting.

Branches in the foliage need special handling. More often than not the main branches in the middle of the trees are different in colour from the surrounding greens, and of a lighter tone. My solution is to paint these branches in first, and then work in the sections of foliage that pass behind them. This allows the light branch to stand out. Some of the foliage will also pass in front of the branch, so if the branch is darker than the leaves, this section of it must be left out. Fine branch detail is best done with a rigger, which can be used with a twisting action to simulate the changing direction of the branch and twigs.

Magnolia trees

Occasionally one is fortunate enough to discover trees that are not green at all. In this case a large magnolia tree, with accompanying flowering shrubs, gave me the chance to experiment with different colours. Because it is a white tree I was able to explore negative shapes, and in this case you have to look for all the various subtle colour changes within the whites. These vary from violets to yellows, golds and blues. I had to use the sky and surrounding buildings to indicate the form of the tree. I have introduced a couple of chairs to give the trees scale and to contrast their natural forms.

Action painting

For me the only true way to paint landscapes is to be confronted with the subject; working from a photograph gives only a fraction of the pleasure. The more problematical the subject, the better I like it; some-how the sheer difficulty means that you have not got time to analyse all the problems in depth, and so you have to draw instinctively on what few skills you have. I urge you to experience as many outdoor condi-tions as possible to develop new ways of seeing the landscape.

Turner inspired me with his notion of being tied to a mast in order to observe the effects of a storm. Similarly, I have painted

Salmon fishermen
This time I wanted to feature the boat in a three-quarters view, and again had little time to do it. I had to employ the white-line technique to enable me to work rapidly, without waiting for drying time. The landscape in the distance had to be seen very simply, the final touches being added before clambering back into the boat again just before the paint had dried. When working like this you need a very large brush that can be drawn to a fine tip, and here I used a large Oriental brush which is perfectly designed to give the desired results.

Hauling the net
Including figures in a landscape is a challenge, as this trio of paintings demonstrates. Careful observation is required before committing figures to a scene. These pictures are the result of intensive study whilst painting the fishermen on the River Dart. I had to transport all my equipment and follow the fishermen as they moved from site to site, casting their nets for salmon. In this study I was concentrating on a single figure acting as a statuesque element, intersecting the horizon line. Because speed was essential (the fishermen would not wait for me) I had to handle the water in a very simplistic way.

from boats; not always a comfortable experience!

Painting outdoors in winter, with your fingers barely able to operate, requires a different kind of brush handling — but how else are you able to study the effects of snow?

To combat these extreme conditions you must make contingency plans. My equipment is always carried in a lightweight waterproof shoulder-bag with a hand grip. I work large, and my board can be a little unwieldy, so I use a sheet of thin plywood, bolted to a lightweight wooden easel. The really awkward item is the water container which holds nearly a gallon (5 litres), but which is essential because I insist on frequent water changes to keep my colours clean. In winter I have a couple of handwarmers in my pocket to keep my fingers flexible, and take a thermos of hot drink, to reduce the possibility of hypothermia. My paper is held flat in a polythene bag, protected by a sheet of card the same size, which I tape to my drawing board. An indispensable item is a roll of soft tissue for painting, mopping up accidents and keeping my palette clean.

The rower
To create a soft, opalescent colour, I used a fair amount of violet. The sky and water were laid in very rapidly. Whilst the paint was still very wet I put in the trees using strong earth colours — raw umber, burnt umber, burnt sienna and Hooker's green. This action was executed at least three times so I was able to study it as a whole before committing myself to the next stage, which allowed the first wash to dry a little. To achieve the main contrast I put in the boat and the fishermen in very strong colour, using the light tones of the water to act as reflections on the boat's clinker-built hull. I just had time to execute the final darkest tones before we had to set off once again.

Colour choice

Landscape with church
The various types of greens in this painting range from absolute blue through to yellow. Some of the greens are very cold, others more earthy.

One of the greatest difficulties in landscape painting, particularly when a lot of foliage is involved, is in handling the amount of green. This problem is emphasised on a bright summer's day, when the sun is high and there are few shadows. The usual course of action is to avoid painting at this time of day, and to pick either the early morning or early evening, when the shadows are long. But this cuts out some of the pleasures that can be associated with landscape painting.

Look for the variety of hues in the green, which can vary from cold, blue greens through to quite warm, yellow greens. These can all be produced by mixing your colours; for example, to obtain a truly dark-blue green, use a phthalo blue with a lemon yellow. This very cold green is perfect for the shadows and detail areas. For earthiness, substitute ultramarine for the phthalo blue. This will give slightly more warmth to the dark green.

For light greens mix a lemon yellow with a cerulean blue (both very pale colours, but with bias towards the yellow-blue end of the spectrum) and the result will be a fresh, spring green. Cadmium yellow is by nature a warm yellow, tending towards the orange. This, when mixed with any of the blues, will provide a more brownish-green, the kind we would associate with late summer turning to autumn. In order to portray the variety of colours in the foliage, it is essential to experiment, and learn to mix these different greens. As mentioned in Chapter 4, the best way to relieve the monotonous greenery in a painting is to use its complementary colour red. At first it will appear that there are no reds amongst the foliage, but look closely and you will be surprised how these reds can emerge. For example, branches and twigs, particularly when dying, will appear as an alizarin red through to cadmium red. The alizarin would emerge from the dark shadows. Dead or dying leaves introduce hot colours amongst the foliage.

A green tree can also be magically transformed to give an almost flame-like appearance when the sun is very low on the horizon. This is due to the sun's rays lighting the back of the leaves and branches.

There is another way to enliven a green painting, but first you must understand about local colour. This is the colour actually perceived with your eye — in this case, the green of the leaves. This colour, however, can be changed in several ways. Atmospheric interference can change it to blue, and the way in which the sun casts its rays on to the leaves, especially if they are very reflective, can change it almost to

white. Constable noticed this and introduced thousands of tiny white flecks, called Constable's 'snow', to create this reflective quality. The leaves can also change to red, as noted earlier, when the setting sun imparts strong red light waves which are reflected off the leaves.

Just because something is there, and it is green, does not mean that you are forced to paint it like that. You can change any colour according to your creative whim.

For example, you may be painting a picture on a slightly misty day, when the distant trees seem to be blue in colour but the trees in the foreground are very much greener. You may wish to 'console' the overall colour of the painting and make it a study in blues. In this case you would introduce light and dark blues, warm and cold blues, with some verging towards violet. Small

touches of complementary orange can be added to give life to the painting. Controlling colour in this way can impart a romantic feel.

Conversely, you may be painting around sunset when the colour red is predominant, and you could suffuse the entire picture with reds, golds and yellows. This would give a dramatic feel to your painting.

Colour control is the artist's choice. Playing with the colour will open up a whole new dimension. Try painting the grass red!

Early morning on the river
I modified this painting to produce an overall cool feel and made everything subservient to blues and violets. The principal blues used here are cerulean blue, manganese which precipitates slightly, and cobalt violet. The aim was to create a romantic feeling.

Foliage patterns

1 I commence by drawing-in, in this case with a reasonably stiff sable brush, but not too small. To avoid the excess of green I use as much colour as possible at this stage. I note, for example, that where the bean poles intersect the greenery they are lighter, but that when they cross over into the sky they appear much darker. To avoid any monotony in the colour I have painted them in varying hues from violets to yellows to blues. When you are faced with so much green, highlight all the other colours you can see, and emphasise the quantity of each.

2 I am now placing much more colour in between the tall bean poles. Having these poles in the way, as it were, means that you have got to treat each of the spaces between them as an individual painting. This is negative painting at its most complex. I have put in patches of colour all over the painting to establish what looks and works best.

3 After the initial laying-in of the primary and secondary colours I am now looking towards the neutral areas, and where possible I indicate some of the darkest tones. For this I use a small squirrel-hair brush, working in and out of all the complicated patterns.

4 It is not until this stage that all the components of the painting start to come together. I now work with a larger brush putting in overwashes and darker tones, to give more life and activity to the picture.

5 Many people tend to overwork their pictures to such an extent that any freshness is lost. In this case I did not want the green to continue to the very bottom edge of the picture, and so deliberately left white spaces to encompass the green areas. This helps to reflect the curved nature of the bamboo rods at the top of the picture, and creates a 'vignette' view of the subject.

CHAPTER 7

WATERSCAPES

I live very close to a large river and the sea, and water is therefore an indispensable part of my surroundings. It permeates the landscape everywhere, in the form of streams, brooks and puddles. Because of its very reflective nature, water picks up all adjacent colours, including those in the sky. Exploiting this characteristic can be very rewarding, and gives relief to many landscape paintings.

The water itself is greatly influenced by the weather conditions, and the effects produced by wind or rain, for example, provide endless opportunities for the watercolourist to practise different textures. We will take the plunge and investigate ways of tackling water in its various moods.

Agitated water

1 Agitated water is about texture, but at the same time it is highly reflective, and will pick up every nuance of the sky colour above it. In this case we are going to lay a wash reflecting a late summer's evening sky — very pink with cool shadows.

The colours used are a pale cadmium yellow with a touch of cadmium red. Cerulean blue is used for the cool shadows. I have employed a soft squirrel-hair brush.

2 In order to imply the reflective quality of agitated water I have introduced some reeds, put in with a broad hake. The reflections from these are broken up, with wider spaces as they come towards the viewer. The colours used for the reeds — a mixture of cerulean blue and cadmium yellow — are the same as their reflections.

3 Where the water gently bends away from the light, it changes imperceptibly to a cooler colour. This needs to be very soft in the distance, becoming crisper as the foreground is approached. The water should be broken up into planes in order to give the feeling of recession. This is done with very delicate cool and warm stripes, which become broader towards the bottom of the painting.

4 It is at this stage I use a soft sponge to blend some areas of colour, and have intensified some of the details in the reeds and in the water reflections.

When using delicate colours such as these it is essential to keep your painting fresh; never let your colours go muddy.

5 The surface activity of the water can vary according to the wind and currents. This ceaseless movement defies the eye to capture it. Basically the solution is the application of textural marks that are ideally suited to the sable and squirrel hair brush. You need to develop the skill of laying down strokes from the tip to the body of the brush, building the texture with smaller marks in the background and increasing their size towards the foreground.

Reflections

1 When painting reflections you are producing a mirrored image. Direct mirror images can look a little obvious and so a little sublety must be used. Here a basic wash is laid in order to set up the scene to be reflected.

2 Whilst the wash is still wet I have the opportunity to manipulate the paint. This involves adding other colours to produce soft gradations.

I am also using a piece of soft tissue to blot and wipe out pigment to produce cloud forms.

3 We are going to use a wet-into-wet technique to produce a bank of trees in the middle distance, and I employ a mixture of reds, greens and oranges. The deliberate flow of the wet-into-wet helps to create subtleties which are a direct result of the lucky accidents so frequently encountered in watercolour painting.

4 The actual trees will be shown in more detail than their reflections. These are now being picked out with a small ox-hair filbert brush, whilst the reflective area is dried with a hairdrier.

5 I have brought in reflected trees in the far distance, whilst the paint was nearly dry. Further details — including branches — are added to the trees, and I have given an indication of the bank. I used my fingernails to scratch horizontal lines on the water surface, which imply the flat plane of the water.

6 The completed painting shows how the reflections have been established by a combination of the colours of the trees above, and certain accents in the water below. The picture has been kept deliberately soft to imply density in the foreground. Finally, some highlights in the water have been scratched out using a scalpel blade.

Calm water

1 The portrayal of water should be tackled in a similar way to the painting of glass. In other words, we will paint what we see through it, remembering that it will be subtly altered by the density of the water.

First of all we need to paint all the objects surrounding the water which will be duly reflected by it, and then anything that exists under its surface. The rocks are laid in with a thin wash of raw and burnt sienna. The stones at the bottom of the pool are put in with varying blue and red sepia colours, and either ultramarine or alizarin is added to the mixture.

2 At this stage the fact that we are painting water becomes apparent. This is revealed by applying a very thin dilute wash of a mixture of ultramarine and cerulean blue to the area covered by the pool. This effectively wraps around the stones which lie three-quarters of the way down the pool showing where they emerge from the water. A broad hake brush is used for this, allowing the colour to pull towards the bottom edge of the paper. You will notice that I have left the occasional white line across the rocks in order to indicate the slightly reflective nature of the water where it meets the stones. The effect of the wash on the pebbles beneath the water is to soften their outlines slightly.

3 In order to emphasise the difference between the rocks under the water, and those out of the water, I now apply details to the ones above the surface. This is a mixture of the same siennas with a little ultramarine to darken the tone. Where the fissures in the rock pass beneath the water surface the line work is kept lighter and softer. I pick out with an Oriental brush all the grasses that surround the pool, darkening them with phthalo green and ultramarine. These grasses play an essential part in creating the reflective nature of the water. Some of them have been scratched out with my fingernail, to leave light grasses against a darker background.

4 To give a little texture to the bottom of the pool I have introduced some splattering, with a varying mixture of raw and burnt sienna together with ultramarine. The splattering, however, is rather harsh and needs to be softened down. Once it is dry, I use my sponge to lightly wipe the surface and thus blend some of these textures together.

5 Needless to say, this is a very tricky subject. Many adjustments to the final effect may be necessary before you are satisfied. It is essential not to overwork a painting like this, otherwise the colours may become muddy and you will lose the vital crystal-like quality of the water.

Water integrated with landscape

The medium of watercolour lends itself admirably to the portrayal of water within the landscape. Many painters in the past have excelled in observing the way in which water reflects and moves; Turner was particularly adept at this, virtually making it his personal domain. When analysing his paintings you will notice that he simplified the water planes in order to create a feeling of impenetrable depth.

It is sometimes extremely difficult to re-create the remarkable properties of water, and to portray these effectively on paper. To begin with, it is very flat and must be handled carefully, or it will look like hills and valleys. The way to tackle this is to introduce horizontal planes, described earlier in the text. Water is also highly reflective, and picks up every nuance of sky or landscape that exists above it.

As soon as water becomes agitated, ripples or waves appear. These will vary considerably depending upon the intensity of the wind ruffling the surface. A very keen sense of observation is essential if you are to paint waves successfully. One of the easiest ways is to freeze their motion with the use of a camera and then simply copy the photograph. However, this removes the excitement that can be experienced while painting them *in situ*.

Ultimately, waves re-occur. First analyse the tonal aspects (locate the very darkest tones, usually on the underside of a wave), put these down, then wait for the sequence to repeat itself. By this method you can slowly build up the painting from each observation.

When painting ripples I find that a No 5 or 6 sable or small-pointed squirrel-hair brush is ideal. You can put down a ripple shape by laying

Moonlight

In order to paint this picture at night I had to pre-arrange all the colours on my palette so that I knew instinctively where they were located. The colours used were violet, phthalo blue and raw umber, and set aside from these I had a pale lemon yellow.

The moonlight was strong, and I could see the surface of my paper quite easily, but the exact colour changes were difficult. The background trees were in fact a very warm, dark blue which is why I used the raw umber. The main focus of interest is supplied by the moon and its reflections, all the whites reflecting on the upturned dinghies, and the pontoon on the left of the picture.

the brush from the tip, down to the body and back to the tip again. Then interlink these marks to imply the way in which ripples appear, rather like fish scales.

Selecting the right colour for water, particularly if it is a reflection, can be very difficult. I have developed a useful trick which will help here: I paint a piece of paper the colour I *think* the water is, and then hold it up in front of the water and see if it needs to be darker or lighter. This is particularly useful when the tones are very dark; these need to be established early, otherwise the colour can become muddy.

I put my surface indications on the water at the final stage — trails in the water, debris or sparkles to indicate reflected sunlight. If these are added too early then the flatness of the water can be lost.

I have always felt that close observation is the most essential part of any painting. If you wish to paint landscapes integrated with water you must study the different moods of water through day and night in order to fully understand it.

Water lilies

This photograph demonstrates the kinds of problem one is likely to encounter with this type of subject. The greens are predominant, and the water is extremely dark in contrast.

We must draw the colour out from the main point of interest, and at the same time note factors like the direction of growth in the plant, and the nature and character of the leaves.

1 In order to separate the leaf forms from the background, I felt it necessary to use a large amount of drawing-in. Because this is a predominantly green subject I have used a light blue (cerulean) for this stage. The brush employed is a fine rigger which gives me a suitable line with which to express the crisp edges of the lily leaves.

2 Dark tones must be established almost immediately. This is a fairly classic example of negative painting, and I have left behind white shapes which will subsequently become waterlilies. In order to obtain reasonably sharply defined edges I have waited for the paint to dry before introducing any of the lily-pad colours. In order to give a watery feel, all the dark background tones have been painted wet-into-wet. I am using a very full squirrel-hair brush which has a fine tip to facilitate working around all the little negative shapes between the leaves. Note that in the background I have introduced quite strong colours to the water, and have allowed these to merge amongst the waterlilies to add some form of vertical emphasis.

In order to bring all the elements together I am washing a mixture of cerulean blue, and changing it occasionally to orange as an overwash. This helps to unify the painting and produce softer edges in the background areas.

You can now see all the various elements drawn together. I have introduced ripples, as described earlier, together with small 'pickings' of light on the surface of the paper which were produced by scratching with a scalpel. An introduction of mysterious orange objects in the left-hand corner gives an added interest in the depth of the water. In a painting of this kind you need to look for as much colour as possible, without disrupting the scene and forgetting that these are leaves lying on a tranquil surface.

CHAPTER 8

LANDSCAPE VARIATIONS

I have painted in many parts of England and all over the world, working with an extraordinary range of subjects, and I never cease to be amazed by the endless variety of landscape available to the artist. Each location offers the opportunity to explore a particular colour or textural theme.

In Devon we are surrounded by rolling hills that echo the cloud shapes in the sky above. Water also plays its part, reflecting and blurring the foliage around it. Vegetation offers a unique opportunity to untangle the complex mixture of greens and shadows. Look for the specific rhythms of a particular view to achieve variety in your work.

Hills

Many years ago I used to be very keen on mountain climbing and I now have an enormous affection for hills and mountains. When viewing the land from a great height, one is acutely aware of the fantastic shapes produced by geological upheavals, and the intricate manmade patterns resulting from farming and cultivation. I still feel very attached to this kind of landscape.

It is an ideal subject for the watercolourist to explore. The classic way to see a succession of hills is to imagine them as a series of cut-outs, like stage flats. The hills in the distance are pale and soft, becoming progressively darker as they advance towards the viewer. This technique is used by many watercolourists. I am fascinated by the particular rhythms that you can see in hill shapes; the way in which the lines of hills weave up and down, linking one top with another in a natural composed way. I liken this effect to the motion in a huge sea.

In more temperate climates cultivation is carried on very high up in the hills, resulting in an extraordinary variety of patterns which vary the texture of the hillsides. These are ideally suited to watercolour brushwork as they comprise of lines for ploughed fields, dots for planted areas, rounded sections for trees and waving lines for crops and grasses. All these dots and lines help reinforce the rhythm of the landscape.

Various hill ranges display different colours according to their locations. This gives you a chance to try out specific colour permutations — the blues and very dark tones of snow-clad mountains, or the red and golden colours of those in the desert. Where hills are tree-covered, pay careful attention to the natural patterning that these trees create.

Hills in the Pyrenees

For this picture I used an absorbent Moulin De Gue 140lb (300gsm) weight paper. This allowed me to work very quickly, placing my brush strokes more as dots and dashes of colour than as a series of washes. The location was very high and the day very windy. I was trying to capture the way the lines of hills meandered and zigzagged back and forth across the picture plane. The colours were predominantly red and green, typical for that part of France. These weaved to left and right across the painting, permeating the whole with a roseate tint. It was interesting to note how the far distant hills appeared almost as cloud shapes. Mysteries like this in a hillscape form lasting images in my mind.

They form almost scallop-like shadows that interlink to provide masses of vegetation. Where trees are shown on the horizon or on the edge of a hill they take up the same tone as the bulk of the land mass.

When composing your picture, imagine the eye meandering between the hillsides towards some far distant objective. The viewer's eye should be led from the bottom to the top, zigzagging upwards to encompass the whole painting.

When setting up a composition for a hillscape I generally go for a high horizon line. The view can then encompass the succession of hills as they march into the distance. A low horizon line is suitable if you wish to paint a silhouette of the hills and place your main emphasis on the sky, particularly if there are very dramatic cloud forms.

When painting on a hillside, be sure to secure your paper. Once, when painting in the French Pyrenees, I was horrified to see my picture whisked away by a gust of wind and float down the mountainside!

Flat landscapes

Beached boat

Mud estuaries provide lots of opportunities for anyone exploring flat landscapes. Small rivulets of water meandering back and forth across the mud add a linear dimension to the composition. This can give activity to the skyscape. In estuaries boats are often abandoned and their forms can be used to give sometimes delicate, sometimes strong, vertical lines to break the horizon.

Here the backdrop of foliage helped to create reflective nuances in the water. This painting was done on a rather damp morning after rainfall, and so I used a wet-into-wet approach.

The first time I encountered a truly flat landscape I couldn't think where on earth my eye could rest. I was confronted with a seemingly featureless wasteland — a dull, grey estuary, with just a few sparse grassy outcrops. My mind could not grasp anything significant in the scene before me. However, I began to notice some specific features.

The first thing that overwhelmed me was the vast expanse of sky. Under certain circumstances the sky can play a very dramatic part.

Rather than begin completely cold I decided to do some research. I could remember Constable's studies of Staffordshire, where he had managed to pick out features and relate these to the flatness of the land in such a way as to give them a poignancy.

Dutch painters also developed a very specific way of seeing flat landscape, and used masts of ships and occasional groups of trees, or an isolated building, to give their paintings great force.

Having absorbed some of these images, the landscape began to untangle itself and I became aware of discreet, but significant, features.

With coastal areas or estuaries of large rivers, the lack of relief gives rise to meandering water courses. Where land has been drained, dams and canals zigzag their way across the area, enlivening the monotony.

With a very flat profile, your picture will have a distinct horizontal feel. Vertical emphasis is needed to break the tedium: elements such as ships' masts, uprights of fences or even the straight lines of grasses in the foreground. Cloud formations can also produce blocks of vertical emphasis where the perspective of the sky reaches down towards the horizon.

A very flat plane can imply a large vista, but if you adopt an extremely low viewpoint you can imagine that you are looking through a portion of the foreground, and seeing the landscape beyond merely as a backdrop. This can create an intimacy of feeling similar to that produced in a painting where the viewer is looking into impenetrable undergrowth. The exciting part of analysing these vast spaces is the interpretation of the planes.

Above The sky can play a powerful role in a flat landscape. The horizon is deliberately kept extremely low, because in reality the landscape itself has very little to offer in relationship to the sky. The power of the skies is almost overwhelming in relatively featureless countryside. To relieve the severity of the horizon line it has been interrupted by one small vertical element.

Centre I have used a very strong vertical element in the middle distance to counteract the flatness of the landscape. This has served to focus the interest, and by using the flat planes of the landscape it has given relief to the drama of the bridge profile.

Below By adopting an extremely low eye-level the foreground can dominate the flat ground, which can be broken in such a way as to link the land with the sky. This picture is reminiscent of Van Gogh's last painting, where the grasses suffuse not only with the sky but also with the crows that have become a portent of his demise.

Seasonal variations

One of life's greatest pleasures is to note the way in which the landscape is painted different colours with the changes in the seasons. These seasonal changes are revealed in the natural vegetation which thrives and regenerates all around us.

Springtime is when I look closely at the ground, and become aware of the magic of colour as it bursts forth from the grey damp of winter days.

Summer is a time for lushness, and my only small concern then is that there is too much green around! The harsh sun, however, produces beautiful light that creates marvellous purple-hued shadows.

Autumn brings the extraordinary phenomenon of all those summery greens turning to their complementary colours of red and gold. Another advantage of autumn is that the sun, being low in the sky, casts very powerful sidelights which produce long shadows. My only regret is that the days are not long enough.

Winter is the season when the trees reveal their beautiful skeletal structures, etched against the sky. It is a time when I play with greys — cobalt violets merging with manganese blue, and umbers mixing with ultramarines. These greys can be used to provide a neutral background to vivid subjects such as brightly coloured buildings. Snow is an infrequent occurrence in my part of the world, but on occasion I will go north and discover the amazing reflective quality, and the way it picks up delicate colours from almost indefinable sources.

My painting seems to change in style, and certainly in colour with these seasonal variations. It is the painter's duty to be receptive to these subtleties and incorporate them in a picture rather than worry about his or her personal style.

Winter snows
I cannot imagine anyone being unaffected by the magic and drama of snow. It is highly reflective, and picks up every delicate shade of colour around. It can show up crisp, powerful, tonal contrasts, and at the same time appear soft and merge imperceptibly with its background. The difficulty encountered when portraying snow is how to prevent it looking too 'kitsch'. In this painting I have taken a small corner by a stream and have examined the strong contrast between this and the hazy flurry of snowfall in the distance.

Autumn trees on the Dart

Autumn gives the painter a wonderful opportunity to utilise a completely different range of colours in foliage. Here we have a varied selection of trees from distance to foreground. I have employed several techniques to create the mass of dense foliage, ranging from splattering to produce the myriad of tiny leaves, to trailing a fine rigger brush for the branches. I have also used sponging for shadows, and wiping to create soft edges. To help complement the warm oranges of the trees I have introduced several tones of cool blues.

Spring flowers

Spring is the time when I concentrate on one of my favourite subjects — the late spring flowers earnestly displaying their foliage to attract cross-pollinating bees and insects. Their colours are so vivid that the pigment makers just cannot match them. For this reason I work large, and give the flowers as much glory as possible.

Trees

1 The most difficult part in painting trees is working out how to express all those leaves, without having to put in every single one. What you have to do is produce a succession of tones that will imply the underlying structure of the tree. For setting down these first basic tones I am using a fascinating brush which produces a very random texture. I am aware that the leaves on this particular apple tree have a way of curving down from the branches, and so the paint is dabbed on in a very free and loose way.

2 When putting down the foliage I am conscious of making sure that the brush strokes vary in size. This reduces monotony. The brush I am using is very much softer than a sable, and is used for placing in the main elements of the tree trunk. I must also remember to leave spaces for where leaves cross in front of the tree trunk. Instead of painting up and down the trunk with the length of the brush, I tend to move it sideways across the surface, allowing sections of the white paper to show through.

3 I have placed a lot of warm yellows over the original washes so as to vary the colour of the foliage. It is now time to work out how to portray all those intricate branches that cross over in front of foliage, and interweave behind it. I have used my fingernail to scratch white lines where light branches would have crossed both the trunk and sections of the foliage. Background tones have been added to emphasise the shape and colour of the trunk.

4 I lay a blue wash over a good 80 per cent of the painting. This wash leaves behind occasional light areas where the sunlight would have hit the top of some of the foliage. This pulls the painting together and helps to homogenise a lot of the white spaces between leaves, and also the white line between the trunk and background.

5 All the details are introduced now. I had fun painting in all the red apples, and showing how the reds changed from quite orange reds to very dark alizarin colours.

Some of the foliage in the distance was softened with background washes and a sponge.

Movement

Everything around us is in motion. In a town or city we are perhaps more aware of the movement generated by ourselves or by numerous manmade objects.

Compared to the obvious human activity in the city, movement in the countryside can be as imperceptible as that of a flower gradually opening, or as dramatic as trees thrashing in a high wind, their branches and leaves flailing against the sky.

We live in a world full of movement and that it is why the cinema stimulated and entranced so many millions when the first motion pictures were produced. Up until that time the visual world was entirely represented by static images in the form of paintings or photographs.

The reason why the moving image has such a powerful effect is that it completely reflects the world exactly as we know it. The painter has a real problem: once a mark has been made on the paper, it is fixed for ever. The painter can, however, try to imply movement in his work to help the viewer relate to the fact that nothing is constant; for example, weather patterns shift and leaves fall.

I first became conscious of how such motion could be implied when I saw the works of Van Gogh. He generated movement with paint by the use of swirling brush strokes and frenzied actions and his paintings induced in me a feeling of great excitement.

Van Gogh was able to make the paint weave in the various elements of the picture, for example, trees sky and ground, in a rhythmic motion. Another painter who also created this kind of energy was Soutine whose distortions in paint conveyed an immense feeling of movement.

Some paintings are intended to generate calm and peace, but even within this apparently static type of picture, imperceptible movement can be implied. What the painter should avoid is that 'frozen moment' look that is inherent in most snapshots. This kind of image

In this preparatory sketch I am exploring how movement can be implied using vertical lines. I do not necessarily mean that you should use dead-straight lines working from bottom to top; let them weave in and out, entwining the colour and merging it with the background. The way in which the paint is applied will contribute to this feeling of vertical movement, as indicated in this sketch of a row of poplar trees.

This is not strictly a horizontal movement but shows a more diagonal one across the picture plane. This sketch, like that explaining vertical analysis, attempts to weave a field of sunflowers through the sky and the background in order to pull the viewer's eye across the painting. Various lines curl back on themselves to generate small vortices such as you would see in a whirlpool.

does not satisfy the knowledge that the sun moves across the sky and that clouds coalesce and merge.

Correct handling of the brush will generate movement in the finished work. Fastidious handling, which merely serves to fill in areas of paint, will never create that electric quality which is needed to make a painting live. We need to analyse the way in which this sense of activity can be implied in brush handling.

One method I have adopted is to work parts of the painting very rapidly, so that I do not dwell too long on the mark that has just been made. Obviously careful brushwork is necessary for certain tricky passages, but by and large you should capture a moment as quickly as possible to avoid the work looking laboured.

It is not only through brush strokes that you can evoke movement. It can also be implied through the use of various compositional devices, as the accompanying sketches will show.

One of the things I always encourage my students to do is stand up whilst working. This allows the whole body to act in concert behind the tip of the brush and in this way your paintings will never look stultified.

Tree rhythms, winter
This painting explores the ways in which you can indicate varying levels of movement. The trees to the left have been painted using a selection of fairly thin brushes. The backdrop and sky, however, were painted with much broader brushes, providing contrast.

There are two different types of motion generated here. The branches of the trees imply movement across the picture, and the stream, together with the path alongside, indicate a movement *into* the scene. This crossover is an attempt to introduce depth to the picture. Keeping the colour very high in key also helps to create a feeling of depth.

CHAPTER 9

BUILDINGS IN THE LANDSCAPE

The imprints that humans make on the landscape are not always sympathetic. Occasionally you will come across a building made from local materials that harmonises beautifully with its natural surroundings, and these are the ones I usually choose to paint.

When we use indigenous materials in our construction, there is an immediate empathy with the landscape. The watercolourist's dream is to find these examples. In painting we are looking for harmony between what Man makes and what Nature provides, and this can be portrayed by careful use of texture and colour. This chapter aims to show how this can be achieved.

Isolated buildings

I am sure we all have an attachment to the notion of an isolated building, be it a home or a place of work — alone in its landscape, yet secure. The appeal of this as an image is very powerful for any painter, and is particularly strong when the building has been constructed from indigenous materials. The fact that it stands alone, surrounded by landscape, provides a natural focal point for any picture.

When considering such a subject for a painting, you have to work out how to integrate it with the landscape. There may not be any defined edges to the building, the ground plane may be broken up by foliage, plants etc, or trees may be growing in front of and behind it. Nature will have conspired to partially envelop the building in some way. It is important to notice this and not let the building stand out like a sore thumb. Consider its colour; it will quite probably have been built from materials locally available, and the colours and textures of these will be repeated in the surrounding landscape. For example, if the building is made of wood, the tree trunks and branches nearby will help to ease the structure into the landscape, and so into the picture. If built of stone, this too will echo in the nature of the area.

There are two fundamental aspects to painting buildings: texture and perspective. You will discover that in order to explore all the textural aspects inherent in the building surface you will need to vary the type of brush used. Brickwork and stonework require different handling, whilst line work for slates requires a fine-tipped brush and so on. I also try to weave my textural marks into the landscape. With perspective it is as well

Lake Palace, Jaipur

This is a very sad painting. The Palace was originally designed to stand in a beautiful lake, but it has now become a ruin, covered with undergrowth that has grown out of an arid basin. I was particularly attracted by the vivid greens that surrounded this pink building. The complementary colours were singing in the powerful noonday Indian sun. Painting this picture was fraught with difficulties due to the curiosity of the local populace, but the details and the way in which the ruin related to its landscape were inspiration enough. This is a good example of how the colour of a building can relate very strongly to the landscape around it when locally available materials have been used in its construction.

to look at your subject straight on, from a distance. This will iron out the awkward angles and be much simpler to paint. A far closer view will create more complex perspective issues especially when the building is seen from a three-quarter-angle.

The building is likely to be the focus of interest in a composition, because of our associations with a sense of home and work place. The positioning of this centre of interest is fundamentally important. The natural inclination is to place it bang in the middle of your picture, but what you must work out is how the landscape itself can direct the eye to it in an oblique and interesting way.

It helps enormously to have an intimate knowledge of a particular building, so it is well worth exploring it in depth before starting to paint. If you are adopting a distant view of the subject, it is still worthwhile getting close to the building to make a few detailed studies. In this way, whatever simplifications you make in the final composition will always have a sense of authority.

The aerial view

It is rare to see paintings with a pre-dominantly aerial view; after all it is only recently that man has been able to fly above the ground and see his world in this way. Looking down on our earth from an aeroplane has always fascinated me, and I find the way in which we have marked its surface — the patterns made by streets, buildings, fields, and hedgerows — particularly interest-ing. Even as a mountaineer I noted the way in which we nestle against the landscape and seek protection from it. Aerial views give us the chance to portray this relationship between the ground and the build-ings imposed upon it.

The first thing you see in such a view is that there is no sky — the land occupies the entire picture sur-face. This means that you need to look at the picture as a pattern form; notice the way in which fields zigzag and streets interlink with each other.

There are several difficulties asso-ciated with looking down on build-ings. First of all, you are confronted with roofs and not much else, so the angle of vision is extremely impor-tant if you wish to give character to any of the buildings. Secondly, if you are in the countryside there is a huge predominance of green throughout the landscape. What is the best way to relieve this?

To start with I take a viewpoint from which at least some of the walls are visible, so that features like windows and doors are discernible and can give character to the build-ings. If working on a country scene I try to refrain from using any green at all by looking at the way in which sunlight affects the surface of the land. I am also acutely aware of how the clouds cast shadows over the landscape.

Autumn sunlight
Near my home there is a steep hill, from which I can look down on to our little hamlet with all its buildings set at various angles to each other. I explored here the effect of a sun setting in the west, which lent a strong, golden glow to the scene. I contrasted this with cool shadow areas to the left of the painting. I applied various washes wet-into-wet over a fairly detailed drawing of the layout of the hamlet. When drawing in the buildings with a brush I deliberately kept the line work fluid so as not to produce too hard a line, and this helped to integrate the buildings with the landscape. You will note that a little three-point perspective was used to generate the feeling of looking downhill.

As discussed in Chapter 3, the perspective of an aerial view requires careful thought. In order to create the sense of height, three-point perspective is necessary and will give a slight looming quality to the buildings. Aerial views actually originated in architectural plans, and were projected from these plans to give the lay person an idea as to what buildings might look like. These were produced by axonometric projection, a method involving no perspective at all. This technique was also used extensively by the Japanese woodcut artists when drawing buildings.

As mentioned earlier, the predominant features in any aerial view are the roofs of the buildings. In the south of France or Tuscany the roofs are very colourful due to the use of handmade tiles which vary in both texture and tone. Slate roofs have a highly reflective quality, particularly when wet. Depicting these kinds of roofs with their higgledy-piggledy angles and planes can produce some exciting subject matter.

Weathered buildings

1 It seems obvious that painting in watercolours in the rain is doomed to failure but with adequate preparation a lot of the work can be done in the studio. In this case, even at the outset, I had a very strong idea as to how the finished painting would look. Because of the complexity of the subject, careful drawing-in of all the component parts is vital. You must then start putting down the main tonal areas in the traditional watercolour method. As you can see, I am moving across the painting picking out sections to see how they will balance in terms of intensity one against the other.

2 I like to establish very dark tones at an early stage in any painting. This prevents the pigment from getting too tired toward the end of the work. Because this is a rather drab subject I attempt to relieve the colour with bright touches of yellow and red. Here I am putting in the ripples and puddles that will be ultimately produced by the rain.

3 The bulk of the buildings and their details have now been painted, together with the fractured stonework. This is the dramatic stage I have been waiting for. I had lightly scored the paper surface to the right with the back edge of a scalpel, so that when this overwash was applied fine lines would emerge, to indicate rain. This overwash had to be executed very rapidly on a gently sloping board occasionally leaving out small white spaces where the light reflected off the roof and window-panes. Sponging out of clouds was also undertaken now.

4 To further emphasise the look of rain, the colours need to be blended in. I use a wet brush lightly dragged over the surface, and add ultramarine with a touch of raw umber to deepen the tone.

I am using a curious fan-shaped brush called a 'blender', which is normally used in oil painting for blending skies or flesh tones. The trailing hairs of this brush are eminently suitable for this work.

5 Further overwashes, principally a mixture of ultramarine and raw umber, complete the painting. I check over for details in the stonework and in the illustration of the windows to add a bit of interest.

Intimate view

1 Twisting, winding roads meandering steeply downhill, with buildings set at different angles, are difficult to paint. It was also extremely cold, so it was vital to work very quickly and with minimum drawing-in. I put down the cool pinks and blues to establish the basic colour theme. Because I had to work fast I am using a very large Oriental brush.

2 I always like to work in the dark tones as soon as possible as this helps me to establish both ends of the tonal range. The white-painted fence in the foreground provides a wonderful opportunity to explore negative painting.

3 The picture is beginning to resemble the actual view. All the basic underpainting has been done, and I am now stressing the areas of walls with slightly darker tones to create shadow patterns and textures. At this stage I use a finer Oriental brush which has good flexibility in the tip.

4 Detail stages are very much a question of balance. Too much detail and nothing is left to the imagination; too little, and the painting appears wishy-washy. In this case because the subject matter is very complicated, the detail is kept to a minimum.

5 The completed painting shows the variety of colour and tone inherent in a landscape of this kind. I wanted to create a definite contrast between the intimate view of the porch entrance and the small cottage on the far bank of the river.

Building complex

A painting which includes a number of buildings involves you in some decision-making: either you try to put in every chimney, window, etc, or you produce some form of generalisation. I take a course between the two.

Give the viewer an indication of the number of buildings, without necessarily providing every shape. Detail areas can then be added to offer a few visual clues, and indicate the complexity of the whole.

If you think of a conglomeration of buildings as a series of hills, where the distant ones are out of focus, the ones in the middle distance have a little more detail, and those in the foreground are even more simplified, you will begin to understand how you can handle such a complicated subject.

You will notice that most building complexes tend to break down into a series of rectangles and triangles, representing walls and roofs. Look more closely at these shapes, and you will see that they are made up of a series of pattern areas. Concentrate on those buildings that will intrigue the viewer. Their relative locations in the picture will give a feel of the underlying topography, and therefore an indication of the surrounding landscape.

Painting a whole series of buildings can become extremely boring, especially if you become too involved with the technicalities. Look for ways to relieve this: smoke drifting up from chimneys, or a particular atmosphere caused by the direction and level of the sunlight. I have found strong light in early morning, or when rain has just fallen, the best times for depicting a mass of buildings. Atmosphere can be introduced which will raise the subject matter to a more romantic level.

Devon village

My local village is situated on the bend of a river. The houses are very old, and climb haphazardly up the side of the hill. The water plays an indispensable part in the life of the village, and is littered with boats. I was conscious of the complexity of the building forms and their personalities. The trees around the village also play an important role. When I painted this picture the light was behind the hillside which made the roofs appear very pale and caused the walls to differ in tone.

Building in a landscape

The photograph below shows the subject in an autumnal setting. Autumn leaves surround the building which is nestling amongst trees. It is just before dusk. I am trying to convey the pattern of leaves and colours that encompasses the building.

1 As with all foliage it is wise to tackle the light leaves first, so as to keep the colours clean and fresh. I am using a soft squirrel-hair brush, pressing down the strokes to create the varied leaf forms. I inject as many colours as possible, from lemon yellow with a touch of cerulean for the very pale, cool greens, to cadmium yellow and cadmium orange for the older, drier leaves.

2 As a colour contrast to the oranges I am deliberately pushing the cool side of the landscape towards the blues and violets. This gives harmony to the leaves and the buildings. At this stage I am keeping the background fairly hazy to create the feeling of filtering light.

3 I am now having to work very quickly in order to retain what little light is left. The various topographical details are added, using an Oriental brush with a fine tip. This is particularly useful for putting in the branches, which twist and turn both towards and away from the viewer. These are added in while some of the paint areas are wet, to diffuse them and to give them greater depth. Others are added where the paint is very dry, and these branches are painted in the darker tones of autumn colours: alizarin, crimson and violet.

4 This shows the final scheme, where the mosaic of leaves has permeated through the entire picture. Negative painting has been employed where blues and browns have been used around each of the leaves, to make them stand out. The stonework is kept deliberately simple so that the leaves show up in front of it. The same method is employed for the house in the background, which echoes the colours of the setting sun and of the leaves. Note that the leaves appear much darker where they break against the sky.

CHAPTER 10

FIGURES IN THE LANDSCAPE

Many people are daunted at the prospect of including figures in their landscapes. The principal difficulty is in the drawing. We are so familiar with our appearance that any inaccuracies show up immediately. Some careful studies are essential before you commit yourself to paper.

Start simply by including only one or two figures in your painting. Once your confidence has increased you can add more figures to the composition.

Past Masters are a rich source of inspiration — in particular Gauguin and Toulouse-Lautrec. These two artists were capable of weaving figures into their landscapes in a wonderfully lyrical way.

Single figures

Whenever I think of figures in the landscape, I remember an intriguing painting by Pieter Bruegel. It depicts a farmer ploughing a field which is situated on a high promontory overlooking the sea. The actual incident of the fall of Icarus (which one assumes is the whole reason behind the painting) is shown as a mere splash in the right-hand corner of the picture. The figure of the farmer, positioned in the foreground, is treated very simply, and yet he acts as the focal point about which the entire composition revolves.

The purpose of a single figure in a landscape is very often to give it a sense of proportion. We can all relate easily to our size, so including a figure gives scale to the trees and other features in the landscape. Because we are naturally curious about ourselves, it draws our interest. The placing of the figure is critical and can be achieved in one of two ways. A very large figure in the foreground will attract the viewer's attention, and its size will enable you to treat it in some detail and explore its character, mode of dress

Tending the vegetable garden
I love vegetable gardens — all those neat rows of lettuce, cabbages and leeks growing in a carefully tended bed.

In this composition I have used the figure as a pivotal point for all the lines radiating out of the picture. I have attempted to enliven the greens by using a rich mixture of blues and yellows. These are complemented by the warm red Devon earth, which derives its colouring from the presence of iron in the soil.

It is important to make the figure look active in these circumstances, so her contours need to be broken to suggest movement.

etc. Alternatively it can be placed quite discreetly in the middle distance. This allows you to handle it more simply, and blend it with the background more easily. This second option is a good one to start with if you are feeling tentative about tackling the subject.

Look at the work of John Constable, who was adept at painting figures in an uncomplicated way. He worked in both oils and watercolour, and was able to imply figures (undertaking all sorts of activities) with very simple brush strokes.

One of my favourite pastimes is to sit in a vineyard in the south of France with my easel and a bottle of wine, making studies of the grape-pickers at work.

The fascination in sketching these human activities is in noting the gestures peculiar to a particular task, and this is especially true when the subject is tending the land. The other advantage of painting people at work is that they have an unselfconscious, relaxed air about them, which makes it easier to portray them realistically.

The reader
The first really bright spring day of the year afforded me the opportunity to take my paints to the beach, and this particular one is noted for its curious and varied rock formations. The rocks are very pale, and reflect the subtle colours that bounce off the sea. The difficulty with rocks is how to establish their size, and I felt that a figure, sheltering from the wind, would serve to emphasise the rock masses.

I like figures to be included in a discreet way, and so the colouring of the figure in this example is similar to that of the rocks resulting in a kind of camouflage effect.

Multiple figures

It goes without saying that portraying a group of figures in a landscape is probably the most complicated of all forms of watercolour painting. This does not mean that you should be put off completely, however — it can be done!

The easiest way to tackle a subject like this is to start by producing small sketches of single figures. You can then add another, and another, and so on, until the composition has been evolved. The time spent in analysing photographs and paintings of groups of people in a landscape is of invaluable help in this complex, but fascinating, area of study.

Painting figures *in situ* successfully involves close observation, and the ability to note down quickly and accurately their various gestures and attitudes. I start with the central character and work outwards from this, noting how some figures appear slightly behind and others to the side of the main one. I build up a mosaic of these figure forms in the same way as I would devlop a series of leaves on a tree. Undoubtedly a knowledge of anatomy helps, but I believe that continuous drawing and sketching is the most valuable lesson of all. It is generally best if you compose your figures around a specific kind of activity; this gives a purpose to the painting, and you will also soon learn that certain motions and gestures are constantly repeated.

There are two artists whose work I would recommend for you to study. One is Canaletto, who used a myriad of figures in his buildingscapes. These were usually standing figures, and were handled very simply. The other is Boudin, who painted many delightful beach scenes. He also portrayed groups of

Fishermen, Goa

I painted this picture in an Indian fishing village. The fishermen had just completed bagging their catch, and were laying their nets out to dry. The sun was very powerful and reduced the shadows to a minimum. I made the central figure the focal point, about which all the others worked. This was painted on the spot with the men moving around, which meant making rapid mental snapshots of each figure, and then drawing-in his position very quickly before any of the colouring took place. Fortunately, some of the groups did not move very much, and others constantly went back to their stations and I could study them more easily. The background was kept very simple so as not to detract from the main interest — the activity of the figures.

people in a simple manner: as patches of colour. In analysing the work of these these two painters you will see how the figures were grouped and viewed as areas of colour, rather than as detailed anatomical studies.

One of the factors you must bear in mind when grouping figures is perspective. It is obvious that as figures move back in space they appear smaller. However, this depends on your eye-level. If you are standing, and all the other figures are also standing, or walking, all their heads would appear level. If you are sitting the heads of the figures farthest away would be much lower than those in front.

My final piece of advice to anyone wishing to explore this fascinating form of painting would be to take up life drawing. Regular practice in analysing the figure can only improve your hand and eye in this respect.

Animals in the landscape

In many respects the inclusion of animals in the landscape presents the same problems as humans. The major difference lies in the fact that animals will not pose for you, and you need to use various devices to overcome this irritating habit. Obviously they pose less of a problem reclining or at rest than if they are actually moving. In early paintings of horses in motion it is evident that artists were incapable of untangling the feet when the horse was moving at speed. It was not until the advent of the camera that the actual motion of the horse could be studied. There were a few notable exceptions to this — George Stubbs in particular — but they were rare. In fact, animal portrait artists of his time (1800s) established the ground rules for the animal portraiture of today. This required extremely thorough investigation of the animal form which even included dissection in order to understand animal structure better. This is an example of the great lengths that some artists will go to achieve verisimilitude in their work.

Animals can, however, play a significant part in a painting when they offer an identity or a focal point. They can emphasise the character and feel of the landscape — large areas of grass seem more logical when combined with cows, in the same way that a desert scene is enhanced by the inclusion of camels. As with human figures, take care that your animals do not

Groups of cows like this are built up from small thumbnail sketches which can be composed and arranged according to whim. The figure was based on the simple silhouette principle, using a sketch of old clothes fluttering in the breeze. The dual interest in the painting creates a certain tension: there is the cow on the right, looking one way out of the picture, and the figure walking out to the left. Note that the black of the cows is made solely from ultramarine blue and raw umber. This can be varied subtly to give both warmth and solidity in the very dark tones. Wiping and slight overwashing help to integrate the cows with the background.

appear overworked within the context of the landscape; they should blend in with their background. Use broken edges to let the landscape 'live' with them.

Their relationship with other figures must be considered in the same way. Try to achieve a natural empathy between the figures and the animals so that the painting has some cohesion. As usual we are talking about the relationships between line, colour, form and tone. With line work, animals are eminently suitable for introducing beautiful varieties: the arched neck of a horse is an exquisite example. All these lines have to be woven in and balanced to create rhythms in your painting, and this also applies to the inter-relationship between the figures and the animals. Simply taking a snapshot of figures working with the animals would not necessarily

work, because the moment will be frozen, and the photograph will not provide a complete understanding of the inter-relationship between the shapes and lines. The best way to overcome this is to make sketch studies of various parts of the animal at rest or as it moves. These sketches can then be used to interact with those of the figures.

As well as detail sketches you can also produce very small, thumbnail sketches of the whole animal. These will indicate its overall shape seen from different angles — three-quarter back, three-quarter front, full front and side etc. This will enable you to compose whole groups of animals when considered either as overlaps or as individuals. This is particularly useful when depicting a herd of cows, for example.

Animals can be quirky — but they can also be fun!

The camel herders

This was painted in Tunisia amid flies and swirling sand. The sand proved rather gritty when mixed in my watercolours! Camels can be rather unpleasant creatures, so unfortunately I had to keep them at some distance — I was just about close enough to examine the textural details, together with the colour of the camels which integrated so well with that of the sand. The only bright note in the composition was the rug on the camel's back reflecting the colours of the herders' head-dresses.

Working in the desert in direct sunlight has its problems — paint dries too quickly, for example. Large brushes, well loaded, should be used and you have to work very rapidly.

If you wish to lay washes, it helps to soak the paper first.

Figure preparation scheme

Many paintings using figures have to be designed. This means that studies must be made before the final composition can be assembled. The genesis for such a design could come from a flash of inspiration whilst out walking, or could be the result of the culmination of thoughts over a period of time. The idea might be based around something purely fictional, or, just as easily, could spring from something observed in the field.

To begin with I execute a few doodles around a certain theme. These are generally very simple, and enable me to determine where there are gaps in my information. If the figure is to be an essential part of the composition, it is imperative to make some detailed studies before attacking the rest of the picture. For this I usually acquire a willing helper — a member of the family, or a paid model. One of the first things I notice is that quite often the intended pose, which seemed quite lyrical in the sketch, turns out to be rather clumsy in reality. This problem can be resolved by making a few quick drawings showing different arm positions, and altering the angle of the head, until a lifelike

Flowers for the table
When sketching a figure suitable for inclusion in a landscape painting I quite often use Conté chalk to discourage me from putting in too much detail. This medium requires broad handling and is suitable for establishing the tones.

To the right of the drawing is a rough sketch of the intended pose. It was interesting to note that the outcome was quite different to what I had originally planned. In this final study I was able to note small subtleties, like the positioning of the hands, which were only possible because I had carefully observed the real figure.

epresentation is achieved. It is at his point that I consider the lighting aspects, which help to establish the ime of day and the overall mood of he picture.

Watercolour painting requires a deftness of touch that does not allow for any laboured overworking. Therefore, I find it helpful to execute a detailed drawing of the figure in its final pose, in order to fix

it firmly in the back of my mind. This means that when I come to paint all the necessary information is available, and the results will come naturally.

Having dealt with the figure (which I always consider the difficult part), I then turn my attention to the landscape. Again I commence with a general view rather than a particular one. I usually have an

idea about the location of the landscape and will probably have already completed a painting of it, for another purpose. Placing a figure within the same context poses different problems.

The colour levels must be established first, and a few brief notes on the scheme are all that is required before the full orchestration of colour takes place.

Conté sketch
This was my first thought about a figure placed in this particular landscape. As different ideas about the colour occurred to me I jotted them down. The basic bones of the composition are there already but, as can be seen, I am not yet convinced about the central figure. Careful studies had to be made before going further.

Colour sketch
It is important to determine the basic colour scheme fairly early on. This must be done broadly, yet at the same time should capture the mood and atmosphere intended for the final picture. In this case I decided to bring the figure very much further forward in the composition.

On the next page you will see how all these various notes were drawn together to produce the final painting.

Figures in the landscape

1 The trickiest part in this kind of painting is the head. This has to be right, for the viewer will concentrate on this area. Once this has been established without putting in too much detail, the rest of the figure can be developed. I try to permeate the colours of the hair and clothing through the landscape in small touches to help integrate the subject into the picture.

2 Having established the figure, albeit loosely, I now indulge in some negative painting to help produce the right contrasts to make the figure stand out. This technique extends also to the flowers, in this case magnolias, which are light against a very active dark background. The daisies are painted in a similar way, with the dark shadows picked out in soft violet greys. To keep the whole painting lively and active I am using a very large Oriental brush which draws to a fine tip. This allows me to get in between all the various flower petals, and at the same time bring in broad sweeps of colour to help tie the painting together.

The background was kept abstract to contrast with the central figure.

3 The whole of the paper is now covered but lacks intensity, and so I need to introduce some darker tones in between the flowers. I refer to these as the 'fiddly bits', where stems pass beneath flower heads and re-emerge the other side. All these details have to be executed with a finer brush. As the painting is quite dry I can also put in branches that appear in front of flowers and leaves to further improve the depth: the red flowers in front of the figure's dress, for example.

4 Working very hard on a painting and concentrating on specific areas will usually throw the picture out of balance. I therefore stand well back in order to assess the spatial relationships. I then commence my dabbing, which may mean brushing light-tone paint over some edges in order to reduce their impact. Alternatively I use my dampened sponge to soften and lighten sections, which also has the effect of pushing parts of the picture, in this case the figure, into the background.

5 Having worked at breakneck speed for the duration of the painting I have to resist the temptation to start fiddling. Deciding when the picture is complete is probably as hard — if not harder — than actually starting. I generally wait for a couple of days to let the painting sit and gel in my mind. Adjustments are made with either overwashes of a pale blue to help unify sections, or by wiping to help lighten and soften areas.

AFTERWORD

Here we have it — a fascinating series of options for painting the landscape, some easier than others. It will no doubt take some time to gather together the experience necessary to go out into the landscape and confront it with confidence but do not let this daunt you. There are other aspects which can give you endless pleasure — simply sitting there and painting what you see. The pure joy of being in the fresh air and discovering new things must not be outweighed by technical problems. Even when you have mastered all the technical knowledge there are other delights in store.

Much of what we seek to express in paint is extremely illusive. One reason for this is due to the thoughts that cross our minds and change and mutate the images we see. These thoughts are the seeds of our imagination and add further colour to our painting.

Imagination and mood

'Your painting is not going to be any good unless you put some "umph" into it,' my mother once said. This statement left me a little perplexed, as I was not quite certain how to quantify this 'umph'! It was obvious from my mother's expression that it was not something that you were able to pin down: you either had it naturally, forced yourself to find it, or it simply was not there. After some discussion it became obvious that what was really needed to develop some kind of atmosphere or mood was imagination.

I could handle imagination — after all, we are all capable of fantasising — but mood was a different question. To understand that I needed to analyse myself.

I am sure that we are all aware that our moods fluctuate and that changes in disposition will affect our work. This can be useful to a painter, but only if you allow yourself the pleasure of exploiting these mood changes. If you are feeling cheerful pick out the bright colours and establish a happy mood; this can also apply to your brushwork or the choice of subject matter. But sometimes you may feel melancholic, and the subtle consequences

Misty morning on the river
There is a beautiful piece of music by Smetana, a Czech composer, that describes a river's journey from its source to the sea. It is highly evocative and conjures up all kinds of ideas about a river and its associations. This music was very much in the back of my mind when I painted this picture, and it influenced both the colours used and the way in which the paint was laid down. It allowed me to get away from the notion that I was simply painting trees and water.

of this feeling can produce the most delicate of paintings.

In a sense we can feed off our moods, and let them instill in our paintings something 'extra' — an element above pure technical virtuosity. Establishing what kind of mood you are in before you start a painting, as part of the compositional process, will help considerably in giving more weight to your work.

I am always amazed at the amount of stimulation that our natural world provides. However, there are occasions when something extra is required in the component parts or point of view, and to obtain this we need to look to our imaginations. It is for this reason that I am never without a piece of paper or small jotter. This allows me to put down whatever bizarre or extraordinary idea that might flash into my mind. These ideas can become the germ of a painting which, together with research information, can become real on paper.

What triggers off the imagination? The other art forms play an important role here; music, poetry and literature have been a wonderful source of inspiration to many artists. A passage of music or a poem can stimulate all kinds of feelings.

Lazy river
Water not only reflects the sky and foliage surrounding it, but also echoes our moods. In this instance the end of summer had induced in me a feeling of lassitude. I have pushed the paint around very gently noticing tiny touches and incidents rather than establishing any firm identities. The painting is very light and the tonal contrasts slight. I was more interested in the way in which the paint was drying and pooling than in trying to make water look like water.

A certain mood can often cause musings of this kind; it can bring about another type of vision.

Having fun

'Life's not all beer and skittles, lad', my grandfather used to say. From the cradle we are urged to treat our lives seriously. The painter, who has to work diligently to unravel the phenomena of the visual world, could easily fall into the trap of becoming *too* intense; if that was the artist's only motivation, there would be no pleasure in the process at all.

Probably the phrase I most often use with my students is 'enjoy it'. If you can draw reasonably well you are quite likely to be a bit of a car-toonist. Painting too should be about experimentation, even in a frivolous way, playing like we used to as children. It is through this fun-loving attitude that we discover new methods of handling paint. It is also our sense of humour that will help us to seek out curious and crazy forms of composition to entice the viewer.

We must remember that we are not painting for the sole satisfaction of the viewer, but also for ourselves. If our irrepressible feelings and sense of pleasure emanate from the work then it is inevitable that the onlooker will share it.

A sunny corner

It was during a childish prank that this scene was presented to me and I noted, then, that it would be fun to have a crack at it.

It was impossible to paint this actual view unless I was a fly on the wall, but with the use of a ladder I was able to make a quick sketch and ultimately compose the resulting picture. The important feeling was one of sheer delight in the profusion of blooms, shown as spots of colour reflecting the tables and chairs, and in the light that permeates through the picture.

Painting has been romanticised to some extent here with the emphasis placed on pleasure rather than on the production of a 'serious' work.

GLOSSARY

Aide-Memoire
A memory jogger (a sketch or photograph).

Aquarelle
A pure watercolour without the addition of body colour.

Axonometric
A form of three dimensional drawing where a plan is set 30–60° then projected vertically.

Body colour
Pigments that have been rendered opaque by the addition of chalk white, for example gouache.

Complementary Colours
Colours which harmonise and are opposite on the colour wheel, for example red, green, blue are complementary to orange, yellow and violet, respectively.

Contre-jour
Against the light.

Cross Hatching
A way of introducing tonal variation by using parallel lines of monochrome or colour. These lines are generally laid firstly at an approximate 45° angle, them overlaid with further lines at a steeper angle to produce a darker tone.

Demi-jour
Half light.

Ferrule
Usually a metal sleeve enclosing the bristles of a brush and attaching them to its wooden handle.

Form
Solid form is expressed in painting by using tonal variations in colour.

Golden section
A system of geometric proportion in which an A B line is divided at C in such a way that CB:AC=AC:AB approximately 8:13.

Gouache
Opaque watercolour paint.

Ground
The surface on which a painting is made, quite often a chalk and glue 'gesso' used for opaque painting like oil, gouache or tempera

Gum Arabic
A resin from various trees which is soluble in water and is used to bind pigments to the paper

Hue
A colour or tint which is either a primary colour or a mixture of colours

Local Colour
The true colour of an object, for example green leaves or blue sky, which is unaffected by atmosphere, reflected light or the mind of the artist.

Medium
The liquid constituent of a paint in which the pigment is suspended in oil or gum arabic and water

Monochrome
Single coloured

Palette
A surface or containers used by painters for mixing colours

Pigment
The basic colour constituent in paint before the addition of a medium such as oil, gum arabic and water

Plein Air
Painting out of doors as opposed to in the studio

Pointillism
A system of applying colour in the form of dots

Polychromatic
Many coloured

Primary Colour
The basic red, yellow and blue. (Secondary colours are a mixture of two primaries, say yellow and blue to make green. Tertiary colours are a mixture of all three primaries and generally produce browns.)

Resist painting
Using substances like rubber or wax which are insoluble in water to resist wet watercolour. Used for highlights and negative painting

Splattering
Using a toothbrush or stiff hog-hair brush dipped in colour and then drawing the fingertip across the bristles to flick random dots of colour on to the picture surface. Areas may be masked off using cut-out newspaper.

Tempera
Tempered powder colour, the pigment is mixed with egg yoke to provide a binder for the powder

Temperature
In painting this denotes a hot (red) or cold (blue) bias in colours, for example orange yellow is a warm yellow.

Tone
Gradations from light to dark in a painting

Wash
A layer of evenly distributed watercolour laid in a series of horizontal overlapping strokes.

Wet-into-wet
A technique of watercolour painting which involves putting wet paint on to damp or wet colour in order that the two blend

Wove
A type of paper finish, so named because of the method of manufacture. The screen from which the paper is couched is a woven mesh.

ACKNOWLEDGEMENTS

Many years ago I was asked to write an essay as part of the conditions for entering Art College. The title? 'Those that can, do. Those that can't, teach'.

I have always been of the opinion that if all artists had kept quiet we would have learned nothing. I do know, however, that to do anything, and certainly to teach, we rely on each other. Without my friends and colleagues this book would not have been possible.

Three of my greatest friends have been the word processor, the fax and the courier service. Without them time would have conquered all. Yet it is the masters of technology who make it work.

Pre-eminently there has been Sally

Christensen 'Oh, she of the nimble brain and fingers'. Stephen Bond, my shadow, all absorbant, who can photograph me *in tempestatibus* both calmly and efficiently. David Porteous, the 'puppeteer' publisher who holds all the strings and has the ability to untangle them. Tina, my muse and mentor who both cracks the whip and protects me from my excesses. Mimi, who keeps the home fires crackling and makes sure that some domesticity survives the pursuit of Art. My children, Mark, Anthony and Lara who always maintain my confidence. I thank you all.

Many of the paintings reproduced in this book have been kindly loaned by patrons and they have my sincere grati-

tude. Mr. and Mrs. Lucas, Lorna Payne, Keith and Liz Harris, Robin and Mary Ling, Ingrid and Patrick Hayklan, Chris Gibson, Lawrence Alkin and my art dealer, Chris Beetles for his encouragement and for the paintings from his gallery collection.

I am indebted to Peter Staples of Winsor and Newton for the information he provided to reinforce Chapter 4.

The paintings by the 'Masters' included in Chapter 1 are through the agencies of the Bridgeman Art Library.

Finally I would to thank Henry Malt of Artist's Choice, also Mert Ransdell and all at North light for their faith in me. Bless them all.

BIBLIOGRAPHY

Turner
by Graham Reynolds
Thames & Hudson

Edvard Munch
by Ulrich Bischoff
Benedikt Taschen Verlag

The Letters of Van Gogh
Edited by Mark Roskill
Fontana

Monet: Nature into Art
by John House
Yale University Press

Constable The Painter and His Landscape
by Michael Rosenthal
Yale University Press

The Basic Law of Colour Theory
by Harold Kueppers
Barrons

Paul Cézanne: The Water Colours
by John Rewald
Thames and Hudson

A Concise History of Watercolours
by Graham Reynolds
Thames and Hudson

The Theory of Colours
by Johann Wolfgang von Goethe
M.I.T. Press

Bonnard at Le Cannet
by Michel Terrasse
Thames & Hudson

Chinese Watercolours
by Josef Hejzlar
Cathay Books

Gustav Klint
by Gottfried Fliedl
Benedikt Taschen Verlag

The Artist's Handbook of Materials
and Techniques
by Ralph Mayer
Faber and Faber

Methods and Materials of Painting
of Great Schools and Masters
by Sir Charles Lock Eastlake
Dover Publications, Inc

INDEX